FLEETWOOD

A PICTORIAL HISTORY

FLEETWOOD

A PICTORIAL HISTORY

Catherine Rothwell

SUTTON PUBLISHING

First published in the United Kingdom in 2007 by
Sutton Publishing, an imprint of NPI Media Group Limited
Cirencester Road · Chalford · Stroud · Gloucestershire · GL6 8PE

British Library Cataloguing in Publication Data
A catalogue record for this book is available from the British Library.

ISBN 978-0-7509-4888-3

Title page photograph: *Fleetwood Docks, 1910.*

Typeset in 11/13.5pt Ehrhardt.
Typesetting and origination by
NPI Media Group Limited.
Printed and bound in England.

Contents

The 1,718-ton Northella, *owned by J. Marr & Son, 1967. The 245ft trawler based at Hull was the biggest ever to land fish at Fleetwood. Equipped with every electronic navigational and fish-finding aid,* Northella *had the first all–metal fish hold.*

Foreword

Catherine Rothwell's book on the history of the town of Fleetwood is a well-researched and fascinating record of the development of the town from its conception to the present time. This book also records in great detail the ups and downs of the development and various projects that have taken place in Fleetwood. Sadly, not enough history of the town has been recorded in one book and now, with the passage of time many great townspeople have passed on, taking their knowledge with them. Therefore it is a great credit to Catherine Rothwell, a local historian and ex-head librarian of Fleetwood's library, that she should have endeavoured to record the history of Fleetwood.

Coming from a well known family, I am delighted to have been invited to write the foreword to this publication, and wish it every success.

Lionel Marr

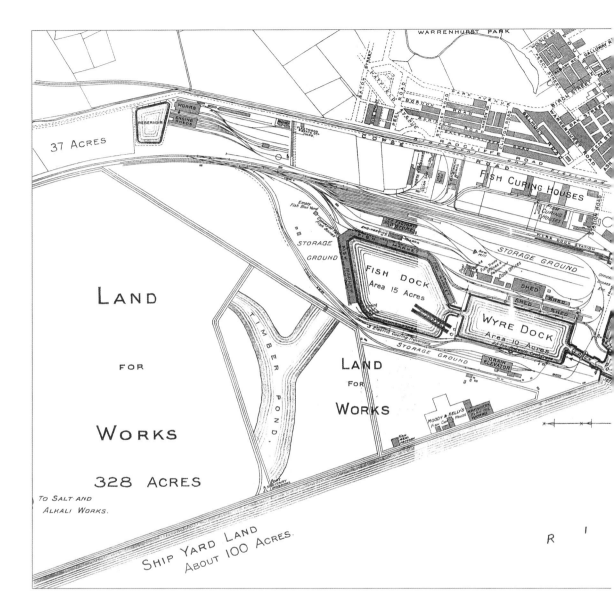

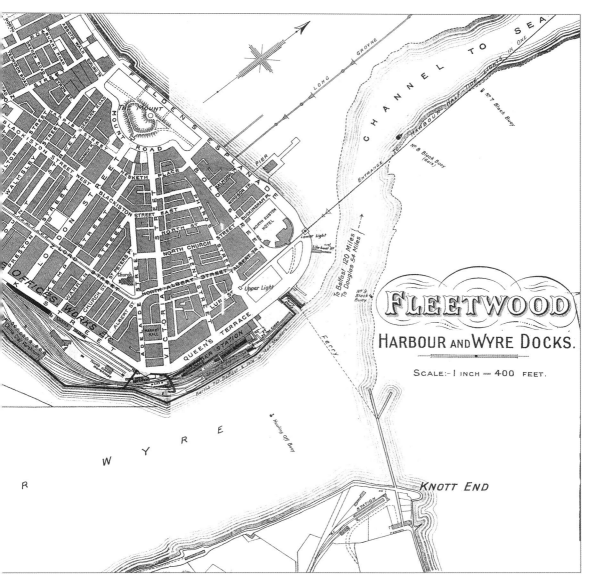

Plan of Fleetwood Harbour and Wyre Docks.

The occasion of the last mayor-making at Fleetwood, when boundary changes had occurred. Left to right: Derek B. Timms, Catherine Rothwell, the Revd Trevor Southgate and Mrs Southgate.

A Note from the Author

Believing that 'history from original documents is like water from a spring with a flavour and freshness of its own', I have tried to evoke the spirit of a town and the character of its founder by handling his original correspondence and the Fleetwood Estate Papers dating from the 1830s.

For this I am indebted to the late Roger Fleetwood Hesketh and Lady Mary Hesketh and for Roger's kindness in reading the proofs of *Fleetwood: A Pictorial History*.

My thanks are also due to Mrs Doreen Lofthouse for friendly encouragement. We share our love of Fleetwood and, as neighbours, we both survived the terrifying inrush of the Irish Sea in 1977.

The loan of valuable photographs from the Lofthouse Co. has enhanced a labour of love, several years in the making. I have also been fortunate in having the interest and excellent photography of Mr Ron Loomes.

Last, but not least, knowledge, so freely passed on from townspeople has been a blessing.

Catherine Rothwell, 2007

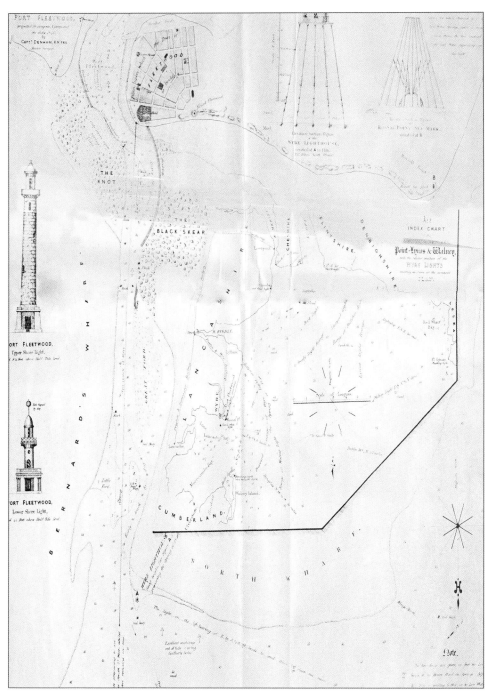

'Plan of the Wyre Lights and Improvements pertaining to Port Fleetwood projected for July 1840 by Captain Denham RN FRS, Marine Surveyor'.

Introduction

Fleetwood's Friends & Fisherman's Friend

When one considers its beginnings in 1830 – two farms, two cottages and a lime kiln – for a town as young as Fleetwood it is amazing how much change, diversity and colourful history has been packed into so short a span.

Having lost much of its cargo trade in 1890, Fleetwood then figured as the heart of a major fishing industry. Then in 1958, when Iceland extended its fishing limits to 12 miles, traditional fishing grounds were lost to us. Additional EEC restrictions and the sad friction of the Cod Wars meant that by the early 1990s most of the port's fleet had disappeared. Not so the spirit of survival born of battles fought in the hard school of experience. Time with its gift of tears could not quench that.

Among benefactors, all imbued with affection for Fleetwood which kept this spirit alive, were Samuel Laycock the Lancashire dialect poet, Benjamin Whitworth,

Benjamin Whitworth.

a rich millowner who provided an Institute in 1863, and the Todmorden philanthropists Samuel and Sarah Fielden. Among their friends was Elizabeth Gaskell, novelist, known for her fearless championing of millworkers' conditions.

Mrs Sarah Fielden, Dobroyd Castle, Todmorden, c. 1890.

Delving further into family history I discovered that a relation, Jasper Fielden, was my grandfather. It emerged that I was eighth cousin in the hierarchy to 'Honest' John Fielden, the member of parliament who, through tireless effort, got the Ten Hours Act through Parliament in 1802 prohibiting children to work any longer than that, daily.

Sam and Sarah Fielden provided a free library for the town and, through their generosity, Fleetwood became one

The Whitworth Institute, 1869.

The engraved stonework above the door of the Fielden Library.

of the first towns to implement the 1850 Public Libraries Act. They also bought a lifeboat, financed the Seaman's Rest in Dock Street in 1899 and opened the Cottage Hospital. On that occasion Sarah spoke profound words, 'In helping Fleetwood we were helping a town trying to help itself'.

Moving to our own times, more classic quotes ring out, 'Who would have guessed that a simple nineteenth-century remedy for the coughs and colds of fishermen would today rank alongside Coca-Cola and Sony as a world-class name with an unrivalled reputation?' They refer to Fisherman's Friend which has brought great benefit to the town of its birth; a dazzling success story first started in a tiny apothecary's shop by James Lofthouse in 1865.

In 1963 Mrs Doreen Lofthouse explored nearby Lancashire and Yorkshire markets and a major springboard proved to be the selling of this super cough lozenge by a Worcestershire branch of Boots.

By 1974 the growth of Fisherman's Friend was such that export markets beckoned – initially in Norway where the cold northern climate and long fishing traditions were the touchstones of immediate success leading to a global brand. Even the citizens of Singapore with its steamy, tropical climate enjoy these lozenges by the million! Duncan, Doreen and Tony Lofthouse, directors of this outstandingly successful company, are Fleetwood's present-day philanthropists.

Today's Fleetwood has had a facelift. Enhanced by nature with its stunning backdrop of the Furness and Lake District fells bordering Morecambe Bay with its rise and fall of the Irish Sea, Fleetwood's promenade has become one of the most beautiful in the land. Winged Eros, poised on an eminence, now heralds a

Mrs Doreen Lofthouse in the apothecary's shop where Fisherman's Friend was first made.

Doreen Lofthouse receiving the Freedom of the Borough of Wyre.

'*Welcome Home*', *Anita Lafford's sculpture.*

WELCOME HOME

Welcome Home
is erected as a tribute to the
families of Fleetwood fishermen who
have down the years shared the dangers and
uncertainties of the industry. Around this spot
families have gathered for generations to 'welcome
home' their menfolk from the sea.

Welcome Home is provided by Fisherman's
Friend with the assistance of Wyre
Borough Council. It was
designed and sculpted
by Anita Lafford.

WELCOME HOME

unique entrance to Fleetwood and no better memorial could honour the memory of Fleetwood's brave mariners than Anita Lafford's sculpture entitled 'Welcome Home'.

Happily sited alongside Sir Decimus Burton's gem, the Lower Lighthouse, this adorable group of figures stands on the spot where it all began; wives, mothers, children waving hail or farewell to their loved ones.

For all this and more (Lofthouse is now the biggest employer in the town) the future looks bright. The future's not orange, it's lozenge!

ONE

Wild Rossall Warren

aria Hesketh of Wennington Hall near Lancaster, wife of Robert Hesketh, gave birth to their fifth son on 9 May 1801, the Melling Church Registers recording the baptism on 10 August. Fate decreed that the boy, Peter, would inherit his father's considerable fortune as his four brothers all died prematurely, one from pneumonia as a result of his own gallantry. In bitter weather on a long journey north, Edward travelled on top of the coach, having given up his seat inside to a suffering passenger. Peter grew strong, long-limbed, enquiring of mind and with a love for his remaining younger brother, which was to be the lodestone of his life. Descended from Sir Paul Fleetwood of Rossall and reaching back through history to Edward II, among family scions were two bishops, two generals, a Recorder of London, a Comptroller of the Mint and a Royal Cupbearer. The family's wealth had been increased by gaining monastic property in many counties and when Peter came into his inheritance on 22 March 1824, the year after his graduation from Trinity College, Oxford, he acquired estates stretching for miles and valued at £450,000.

Wennington Hall, birthplace of Peter Hesketh, who became Peter Hesketh Fleetwood, founder of Fleetwood-on-Wyre.

Fleetwood under construction. London Street leading to the docks, 1836.

Rossall Hall looked out onto a small community of white-washed buildings. Beyond rolled acres of treeless pasture with small farms hugging the 'holmes' – Larkham, Fenny, Flakefleet, West and East Warren Houses, Carr Houses, Fleetwood. Inland, the flatness of the horizon was broken by the outlines of Bourne Hall and Marsh Mill. In this area ruled by the winds, there was even a windmill on Rossall shore. What few stunted hedges existed were weirdly bent by prevailing sea-wind topiary. In that same year the bleak Warren, which harboured rabbits, hares, oystercatchers and herring gulls in their thousands, was valued at just £59. Sandhills tufted with marram grass and starred with sea pinks, sea lavender, sea holly and evening primrose bordered the shingly beach. The wooden landmark at Rossall Point had been placed there by the Lancaster Commissioners to guide their ships. On clear days across the bay were visible what Captain William Latham's contemporary sketches called the Northern Mountains, and as the eye looked inland, the steel-blue hulk of Bleasdale Fells.

The many variations of its name, Rossal, Rushall, Russal, Rosso, echo a long history. Proof that the area was once thickly forested is shown far out at the lowest tides' reach where remains of a subterranean forest can still be seen. In spite of occasional dramatic deluges of seawater (whole villages have traditionally been swallowed up on the Fylde coast) out of Rossall Warren was to blossom Fleetwood-on-Wyre.

At the age of twenty-four, Peter Hesketh became owner of nearly one-third of the coastline between Formby Point and the mouth of the Wyre. Preston, hub of Lancashire and the cradle of the Industrial Revolution, was quickening with a flow of trade unprecedented in its history. Cities like Manchester, in a hideous sprawl of hurriedly flung-up houses, were hiving together hundreds of people – cheap labour for the mills.

To be possessed of such wealth in the heady atmosphere of the Industrial Revolution's gathering momentum must have been both exhilarating and daunting. Almost every technological advance was then coming from Britain and Queen Victoria was sovereign over a quarter of the globe.

Riding, hare-coursing and practising archery in the great field at Larkham, Peter would see the fine natural harbour and call to mind that inseparable comparison old as the hills 'safe and easy as Wyre Water.' Clean, firm sands and the glorious scenic background of Furness and Lake District fells skirting

Marsh Mill, 1794.

Morecambe Bay would remind him that not 20 miles from this vigorous coastal air, trade was booming where white-faced workers endured long hours, sickness, and appalling housing conditions. The majority had never seen the sea and although holiday resorts were springing up all round the shores of Britain and Dr Beattie was to make his celebrated tour of them accompanied by an illustrator, as yet there was no true development on the north-west coast.

Railways were the wonder of the age. Even the queen was impressed. The bringing into being of a town, especially one situated on a remote peninsula, demanded a railway. These early years were the happiest in Peter's life and a forcing-ground for his ambitious plan. He sailed on the Wyre to assess its possibilities; frequently he tramped the Warren through sand and shingle as the exciting idea of building a port and watering-place took shape in his agile mind. Lancaster and Preston had silting harbours. A new commercial outlet for the expanding north-west was badly needed, and on his own estates was both a time-honoured harbour of refuge and a pleasant, healthy retreat. There was opportunity in the venture to promote science and progress to which he was very much alive. It was already apparent that speedy communication between London and Scotland was vital, but it seemed unlikely that a rail route would ever be made over Shap Fell. Sailings from the new town to Scotland, Ireland and the Isle of Man were a certainty. His cherished ideals and ideas, still castles in the air, were poured into letters to his brother Charles. Throughout the course of his life Peter unburdened himself this way and in these documents the whole brief enterprise with all its poignancy is revealed.

On 8 June 1826 Eliza Debonnaire, the beautiful niece of the first Governor-General of Canada, became Peter's wife and they spent their honeymoon in Dover at Maison Dieu, a house still in existence. Peter bought a sand yacht and had it conveyed north, the first of its kind to whizz along the miles of golden sands now famous all over the world, especially the Blackpool stretch. His tenants loved him. Vincent St John Beechey, a son of the famous portrait painter and the first incumbent of Fleetwood parish church, said of Peter, 'in the cottages there was a halo round his character.' A poem dedicated to Peter by John Lennon, a Preston handloom weaver, contains 'their prattling offspring lisp his praise.' Debonnaire became as popular as he at county dinners, regattas, shooting contests, but her delicacy was soon apparent and the death of their first two children cast a swift sadness.

Peter watched with great interest the opening of the Liverpool and Manchester Railway on 5 September 1830. In the same year (on 6 March) his lavish sense of occasion had expressed itself characteristically in a mile-long flamboyant precession. As High Sheriff of Lancashire (a position regularly held by his ancestors on both the Hesketh and Fleetwood sides since Elizabeth I) he was to have escorted the Judges to the Lancaster Assizes. Grey horses drew his carriage;

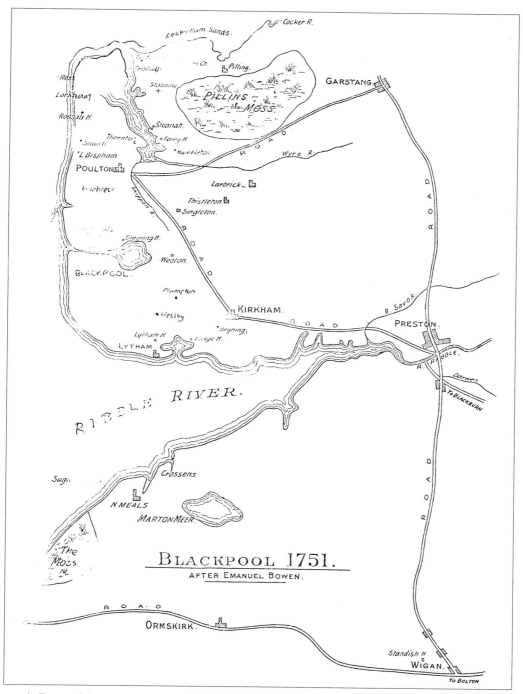

A. Emanuel Bowen's map of 1751, showing Rossall Hall and the ancient farm Larkham, but no Fleetwood.

outriders wore blue and scarlet; tenants attired as javelin men and trumpeters rode white horses, as did Peter himself. His favourite White Arab stallion was painted in 1828 by James Ward RA and the life-size canvas exhibited. The ancient churches of Poulton and St Michael's set their bells ringing joyously across the Fylde as the procession wound on to Garstang where forty guests dined at the Royal Oak Hotel and the rest were well provided for elsewhere. Joined by others from Preston, they moved off again, but because of the difficulties of travel one judge did not arrive until the following day (when the Revd Charles Hesketh preached a sermon) and the second not until Monday – an early instance of how Peter's best-laid plans seemed dogged by misfortune not of his own making, an instance too of his integral, boundless generosity in the days when he had 'too much and to spare.' No thought then of days when he would ponder over a postage stamp.

Between 1832 and 1847 he was the Member of Parliament for Preston, sincere and magnetic enough to head the polls. In debate he was a force to be reckoned with, remarked upon by Lord Melbourne, Sir Robert Peel and Lord John Russell, but ill health cut down his attendance in both houses, 1833 being the most cruel year of his life. The seeds of consumption in Debonnaire quickened. Following the loss of their son and heir and 'a second dear babe' she gave birth to Frances. Just three months later when the family were in London, Debonnaire became seriously ill and, aged only twenty-six, died on 10 January. Worse was to follow. Two weeks later Peter contracted scarlet fever, which in those days was a killer disease. Combined with this was jaundice and erisypelas which cost him the sight of one eye. Doctors said they had never met such a case and while the fight continued for his life the infant daughter died from measles. Charles came down to watch by his bedside with Peter's brother-in-law, T.J. Knowlys. Of these calamities Peter wrote twenty years later, 'There is about that time an indistinctness of memory that was the natural consequence of the jar on my nervous system by four reiterated strokes of death to those most dear to me.' He begged Charles not to come for fear of infection but it is Charles's letters home to his wife that reveal the dreadful progress of events at 24 Hanover Square. It was Charles who planted a last kiss on Debonnaire's brow 'dear, dear Peter may God preserve you to us, we watch for any symptoms resembling Debonnaire's.' By June Peter was up and about, but the year 1833 must have been engraved on his heart and the unutterable sorrow of those tragedies never left him. Even the elements conspired. On the last day of the old year severe flooding damaged his estates. Cattle and deer were drowned, sea defences breached; the park of Rossall never recovered. He was forced to be absent from parliament and to shelve his cherished plans, but he emerged into public life a saddened, not embittered man. Determined involvement in railway and town building was a sane means of fully occupying his mind. He travelled abroad with friends of Debonnaire who

Rossall Hall, 1840.

understood and respected his silences. He made a business trip to Calais, Ostend, Bruges, Ghent, Coblenz and Frankfurt. The flooding had delayed site inspection plans, but his determination to continue in spite of everything led to the first step being taken in 1834 when a meeting was held in Preston at the Bull Inn and resolutions were made to raise capital to build a railway from Preston to the site of the new town. The Friends of the Preston and Wyre Railway and Improvement of the Wyre Undertaking, with Peter Hesketh Fleetwood in the Chair, unanimously agreed on the three major proposals in November 1836. By Royal Licence in 1831 he had been allowed to adopt the surname of Fleetwood in addition to his own.

At this point it is interesting to note an alternative proposal to develop Rossall Warren. In an undated letter from London he wrote to his brother, 'I seldom do anything of importance without telling you . . . I have been applied to respecting a fishing village at Rossall and a farm of 1,000 acres on long lease.' The applicant was Robert Owen, nineteenth-century industrialist and founder of the New Lanark community, a system of division of labour based on the principle of collective farming. In Rossall's case it was also to include fishing. Peter showed customary tolerance and sympathy but staunch Church of England man that he was, he rejected Robert Owen's request 'his religious opinions are vague and not mine. Owen is said to be a visionary philanthropist.' Ironically, time was to prove that Peter would also be set down as a visionary but with none of Owen's flair for success. In the spring of 1836 the first sod of the new town was cut. The scene must have resembled some outpost of the British Empire. A small group of interested people including tenants, gathered round. The site was to the South Bank of the Wyre at Burn Naze where later stood the massive ICI plant. Underneath the foundation stone were placed coins of the realm and as the cheers were blown away on the gusty air of the salt marshes, proudly waving above was the Union Jack.

One child now remained to Peter, but not for long. Mingled with much involvement in business, parliament, electioneering, civic and judicial occasions, the forlorn thread of his grief runs through all his correspondence. 'Tomorrow is Sunday, to me a melancholy day, the anniversary of Debonnaire's death,' and a friend reported 'his mind is much affected by the time of the year when the first heavy afflictions came upon him.'

Peter Hesketh with Anna Maria, the surviving child from his first marriage.

The entrance to the Fleetwood Hesketh family vault at St Chad's, Poulton-le-Fylde. It was here that the embalmed body of Peter Hesketh's daughter, Anna Maria, was brought from the London house. The worn Latin inscription translates as 'The arms of Richard Fleetwood, parton of this church, 1699'. (Ron Loomes)

Part of the Fleetwood Hesketh family pew in St Chad's. The original was so large and took up so much space that in subsequent years, when alterations were being made to the church, it was reduced in size (about 1750). Note the double-headed eagle and the wheatsheaf, both part of the family's crest. (Ron Loomes)

The church of St Chad, the tower of which was built in 1648. In the foreground is the cross which once marked a Poulton boundary. Only the steps are remaining from the original Cross. Peter Hesketh owned the advowson (right to appoint clergy) for St Chad. (Ron Loomes)

The armorial bearing and date 1636 refer to the landowner Sir Alexander Rigby of Layton, then in the parish of Poulton-le-Fylde (although at that time it was called Pulton). The '-le-Fylde' was added when the Penny Post began, to prevent local post mistakenly being sent to the village of Poulton-le-Sands. This dated gate entrance is also part of a pew belonging to the Rigby family. Sir Alexander had a townhouse in the marketplace near the church. (Ron Loomes)

May 28th 1835 – to Charles – 'another anniversary . . . this time is to me a blank, heavy oppressive time and I feel chilled when thinking on it . . . I am not as resigned as I ought to be.'

Anna Maria, the only child to survive infancy, died when she was eleven years old in 1838, the same year in which Peter was created a baronet. Symptoms of the disease that had claimed her mother began to appear. In the last few weeks of decline her father never left her, sleeping alongside and attending personally to her wants. Following her death, Anna Maria's body, in her favourite pony cart,

The bells of St Chad's, hung in the belltower. The tower was built about the time of Charles I's execution. Among the numerous signatures ordering Charles I's death was that of Sir George Fleetwood who became a general in the service of Gustavus Adolphus and later the Swedish ambassador to England. The bells were rung when Peter Hesketh, appointed High Sheriff of Lancashire, laid on his lavish processional to Lancaster Assizes in March 1830. (Alison Callum)

Hatchments on the walls of the gallery in St Chad's. One dates from the reign of George III. Others relate to persons of noble houses whose coat of arms would be hung outside the manor house for several months after death, finally to be moved inside the church. This could be a Veale, Hesketh or Fleetwood family hatchment, which originally hung outside Rossall Hall or Rossall Grange. (Ron Loomes)

travelled from London to Poulton-le-Fylde where, in a coffin with a glass sheet within to cover the embalmed body, it was placed in the Fleetwood Hesketh family vault at the parish church of St Chad. Peter travelled with it and on arrival at Rossall Hall wrote 'The Mourner's Return' adding 'these lines written after accompanying the remains of a loved and last child from London to the family resting place in Lancashire were intended merely for private perusal among those interested in the beautiful, too highly gifted deceased.'

TWO

Supported by Spirited Funds

Following Anna Maria's death, loneliness and a feverish restlessness expressed in letters to Charles seemed to drive Peter on so that he plunged neck and crop into plans for the new town and railway, often wearing himself out in the process.

October 7th 1838 – 'If you would give instructions to place £4,000 of the money to my account with Drummonds . . . I am anxious for the money as I had made some railroad arrangements calculating on this sum . . . I have been walking over the slutch and sand all day. I got a tumble and half dislocated my shoulder on Thursday but it is well so far except very weak.'

October 28th 1838 – 'I only reached Rossall at eleven last night On Wednesday I shall be at Preston and dine with the Mayor.'

November 5th 1838 – 'Do you think you can come next week and dear Anna and any others you like to bring and we can look and talk about all things here, for my dear brother, on you will devolve all the perfecting of my ideas . . . the Colonel has increased his estimate from the original one of 130 to about 230 thousand, a slight difference . . . which puts us rather on our backs . . . as he just took a pinch of snuff as composedly as if nothing had occurred . . . the sooner you come and the longer you stay, the better.'

November 8th 1838 – 'I shall return to Rossall by Thursday or Friday and I should like to have you there dear Charles as much as possible.'

The correspondence of two years previous also reveals much planning activity, negotiating and travel. Frederick Kemp, son of a Norfolk farmer, acted as Peter's steward. The route of the railway was laid out and any land on the route not belonging to the Lord of the Manor had to be purchased. As far back as 1830 the committee from Preston came out to view the river area. Travelling via Thornton and Burn Naze, East Warren Farm and the Nepps (the borders of Wyre

*Preston and Wyre Railway marker
stone for the Preston to Fleetwood
railway route.*

uncovered at neap tides) they passed over the Warren, meeting Peter who came
out from Rossall Hall. In a large sailing boat they travelled as far as Skippool and
Wardleys, the ancient harbours which had long received ocean-going vessels from
Russia, the Baltic and the West Indies. Other claims and other sites were put
forward for the new Lancashire port, but it was small wonder that the committee
accepted the magnanimous offer of Sir Peter Hesketh Fleetwood. He was willing
for the railway to pass through his lands without any remuneration and to pay half
of its costs. At the terminus he proposed to build quays and warehouses in a
planned town comprising health resort and port. The choice of Wyre from the
start brought volleys of criticism. Speculation-mania was in the air but the
country as a whole was poorly funded. Parliament put through a Bill insisting that
four-fifths of the probable expense of a proposed railway should be subscribed
before the Bill was read, thus avoiding a waste of their time in the general
scramble to promote Bills. As Peter's scheme was soundly backed by his own
income and the flat Fylde declared ideal for railway building, a start could
confidently be made. The Preston and Wyre Prospectus and Plans carefully
explained every aspect and stressed that the project was intended to develop the

commerce of Preston. Unfortunately, however, the people of Preston were not at all sure that a rival port set up by one of their representatives in parliament was a good idea for their town. Peter came in for criticism and abuse exacerbated by the fact that he sold out all his shares in the Ribble Improvement Scheme to those with more confidence in that project. He was convinced that of the two rivers, the Wyre was infinitely superior and history has proved him right. The main drawback was distance from Preston but it was countered that swift transport would effectively close the gap. More favourable country for railway building would he difficult to find, said Colonel Landmann, 'the whole length, 17½ miles, may be made without interfering with any park, ornamental or villa grounds. From 4 King William Street, London, on 9 June 1335 he stated, 'I estimate that the Expence [*sic*] of Making a Railway from the Borough of Preston to Wyre together with the proposed improvements in the Harbour of Wyre all in the County Palatine of Lancaster at the sum of £122,000.' The Civil Engineer's mistake in this original estimate was to prove disastrous in the affairs of the founder of Fleetwood, or 'New Liverpool' as it was termed.

At the stone-laying ceremony on 7 April 1836, the commercial end of the town was named Wyreton and at an important meeting at Rossall Hall at which conferred Decimus Burton, the architect, Landmann, Kemp, Lewis Cubitt, railway architect, and Owen Tickell Alger, lawyer, decided that Fleetwood should be the name of the resort. Engineers Bushell and Vine surveyed the track; the contractor George Stanton handled bridges and permanent way between Burn Naze and Tulketh Brow, this section being reported complete on 2 February 1840, but the construction of the Embankment from Burn Naze to Cold Dubbs terminus proved very difficult because it crossed the salt marshes at Kirkscar Bay. It was hoped to reclaim this area of land, enclosing it by the railway, but no contractor could keep the sea out despite 3,000 tons of rubblestone delivered monthly. By July 1836 large quantities of materials were coming from Heysham and Arnside in sloops; powerful horses were being used. Vessels came to Skippool loaded with barrows, wagons, picks, shovels, measuring instruments and rails. The Embankment proceeded with a base laid of 500yds by 30ft; 10 buoys were placed in the

Sir Decimus Burton, architect.

The Timber Trestle from where the first Preston and Wyre trains ran, 1836.

river to mark safe entry. Three hundred men and forty-five horses were working day and night but the attempt to reclaim the marshland was unsuccessful. In 1839 storms breached the Embankment and much of the stone was washed away.

The directors brought in Joseph Locke, the railway engineer, to inspect the line and check on Landmann's figures. He discovered that the total cost was to be nearer £300,000. Notice then had to be given to parliament for powers to raise further capital. With more help from Sir Peter Hesketh Fleetwood it was decided that £85,000 in addition to the original capital should suffice. Tenders for an amended Embankment were invited with the stipulation that it must be finished by June 1840 and further powers sought for a cutting near Poulton where the line was to be diverted. Beside five engineers, George and Robert Stephenson were appointed to supervise, and a timber trestle intended only as a temporary measure was finally used for the troublesome Embankment. At the end of the trestle section was built Fleetwood's first railway station opposite the Crown Hotel in Dock Street. Stations along the route were Lea Road, Salwick, Kirkham and

Poulton. 'We have let the Viaduct Preston to be completed by the 15th July for four-teen thousand and a few hundreds,' wrote Peter to Charles, 'the rest of the line will be ready and then I can rest from my anxieties . . . I am still in London on the Preston and Wyre business . . . I hope to see the railway finished in another year, I hope, and then very happy I shall be for rest and quiet. I am grown thin and perhaps not so strong-looking. I have had so much more to layout than expected and in every way been compelled to give up much in order to expedite and satisfactorily complete the undertaking.'

On 22 February 1840, the stretch of line between Burn Naze and Tulketh Brow was declared complete, but tragedy struck when the ninth of the fourteen arches between Tulketh and Maudland was being completed. Arch and scaffolding suddenly collapsed, killing eleven bricklayers. On the whole route the Viaduct and Embankment were the only works of engineering importance. During 1839 and 1840 there was much activity in Fleetwood itself. Five streets, four rows of cottages for workmen, two lighthouses and a gas works had sprung up.

On 9 March 1840 Peter again wrote to Charles, 'I have placed the railway in a position to open and under the blessing of God the place I have given my name to is beyond the risk of non-completion.' There is a letter inviting Charles to the opening ceremony. 'Tell Anna, ladies are not asked to the luncheon at Fleetwood, but she knows I shall be very glad to see her at Rossall.'

On 15 July 1840 – the long-awaited day, there were joyous scenes in Fleetwood. People from all over Lancashire gathered in the infant town itself and along the route of the railway. A large crowd assembled at Tulketh Brow, for it was rumoured that as the first train rumbled across, the bridge would surely collapse, and what a gruesome tale to tell to the grandchildren. At ten o'clock, an engine appropriately named *Fleetwood*, with four carriages, took Sir Peter Hesketh Fleetwood and friends to Preston to meet the directors of the company. Several accounts appeared in the press – *Lancaster Guardian, Manchester Guardian, Preston Chronicle, Preston Pilot* – from which it is apparent that 3,000 people assembled at Fleetwood to greet the train when it returned. A *Manchester Guardian* announcement had stated that the North Union Railway would be providing locomotives and carriages for the Preston and Wyre Railway (22 April 1840), and the *Preston Pilot* account of the opening describes the long special train which left the North Union railway station, Preston, at 11.50am, as being pulled by two engines *North Union* (probably *North Star*) and *Duchess*, scheduled to arrive in Fleetwood at 12.50pm. Boylike, Sir Peter travelled in the engine. A public holiday had been declared in Kirkham, where the train arrived at 12.15pm. Seething crowds jostled around stalls and booths. The decorated train had left Maudland to the strains of assembled bands and cheers. There were more ringing cheers as it sped on to Breck, Poulton, and finally a tumultuous reception at Fleetwood.

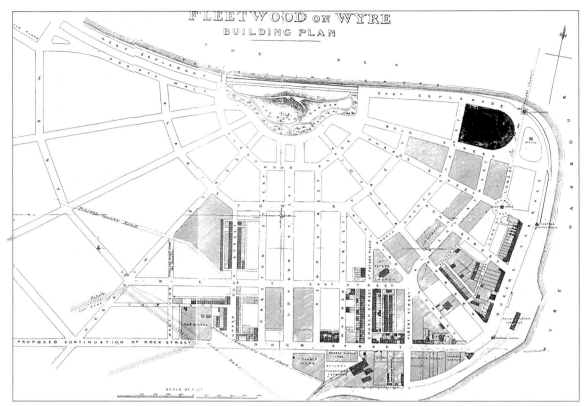

Decimus Burton's plan for Fleetwood, 1841.

The steamers *Express*, *Cupid* and *James Dennistoun*, owned by Sir Peter Hesketh Fleetwood, were moored ready to take trips round the bay, viewing the new Screw Pile Lighthouse and at 3 p.m. four hundred men sat down to a generous feast at the new Station House. Above their heads floated a blue and gold banner, 'England's greatness – Labour and Capital.' There were loyal toasts to the Queen, Prince Albert, Sir Peter and so on right down to the labourers on the line. Emotional speeches marked the culmination of years of work. Among the guests were men connected with the town and harbour; Captain Henry Mangles Denham, George Stephenson, Daniel Elletson. To Sir Peter's great joy, his brother Charles was there, with many other clergymen and great landowners of the Fylde.

People took the opportunity of viewing the layout of the new town from the Mount. Unfortunately the day was marred by tragedy. When the seven o'clock train left for Preston, a foolish passenger, worse for drink, tried to change carriages as the train crossed the Embankment, and falling he was decapitated.

An account of this incident, reckoned a bad omen by some, appeared in the *Lancaster Gazette* on 18 July 1840.

In that first month 20,000 persons were carried by rail instead of the expected 15,000 per year. 'I need not tell you how well the railway works, nor the hundreds who go by it' (30 July 1840). Peter to Charles again (19 September 1840) 'This last week our traffic has kept up surprisingly near four thousand. It does quite astonish all who witness its success. I think that my Prestonians are beginning to take an interest and many are going to look for houses next weekend.'

Wonder and astonishment continued. The very first issue of the *Fleetwood Chronicle and Monthly Advertiser*, on Saturday 11 November 1843, printed the following poem under 'Original Communications.' It contrasts real horse flesh with the iron horse. Written under a pseudonym 'First Class' it is highly possible that Henry Anderton, Fleetwood rhymester, who was charge of the first railway station, wrote this. The inimitable style is there!

Railways and Other Ways

Some fifty years since and a coach had no power
To move faster forward than six miles an hour,
Till Sawney MacAdam made highways as good
As paving stones crushed into little bits could.
The Coachee, quite proud of his horse-flesh and strip,
Cried, 'Go it ye cripples!' and gave them the whip.
And ten miles an hour with the help of the thong
They put forth their mettle and scampered along . . .
. . . coaches alive go in sixes and twelves,
And once set in motion, they travel themselves.
They'll run thirty miles whilst I'm cracking this joke,
And need no provisions but pump milk and coke.
And with their long chimneys they skim o'er the rails
With two thousand hundredweight tied to their tails!

On 9 November 1844 the *Fleetwood Chronicle* proudly printed under 'Preston and Wyre Railway': 'In accordance with the Act passed last session in Parliament for providing cheap Railway Travelling for the more humble class of society this company commenced running their penny a mile trains on Wednesday week. What will our railway friends over the water think of this?'

The Preston and Wyre was among the earliest railways formed. When the 'iron horse' flew across the Fylde it meant the farmer could send his produce to Preston besides Kirkham, Poulton and Garstang, which hitherto had been the only towns available. The carting of heavy commodities, like coal, was solved.

Single fares at commencement were Preston–Fleetwood 1st class 4*s* 6*d*, 2nd class 3*s*, 3rd class 2*s*. The directors decided to run 3rd class carriages for poor folk expected in the summer months and an agreement had been made with the North Union Railway to supply locomotives at 2*s* 4*d* per mile, per train.

Sir Peter had sampled railway travel frequently. The *Preston Observer* of 16 February 1839 reports him as a traveller by North Union Railway on 14 February between Preston and London. Did he, on this occasion, switch eyes? Roger Fleetwood Hesketh relates from family annals that 'great-uncle Peter' following the loss of his eye, had a set of glass eyes made, among them animals' eyes and as the train passed in blackness through a tunnel, he would change his own glass eye for one of these, and watch the result as the train charged forth into light. The effect was frequently devastating. Sir Peter's macabre sense of fun may have stemmed directly from his suffering, or it may have denoted a capacity to turn even tragedy to account. In a truly wizard mood, to heighten the effect still further, he was known to drape a handkerchief over his good eye.

THREE

The Wyre is a Good, Safe River

'The survey of Morecambe Bay is entirely charted in the accounts but two thirds of the cost will be defrayed by Sir Hesketh Fleetwood, our worthy Chairman, who in this as in several other instances spontaneously offered to relieve the Company's expenditure.' This survey, undertaken by Captain Henry Mangles Denham, who was employed to improve the harbour, is referred to in the October 1842 Report of Frederick Cortazzi, Managing Director

The entrance to the Wyre at low water, 1836.

Waverley, *the last of the paddle-steamers, churns the waters of the River Wyre at Fleetwood fresh from the River Clyde.*

to the Board of the Preston and Wyre Railway Harbour and Dock Co. The original idea was that the improvement of the harbour should be run as a separate undertaking, but railway building troubles led to the amalgamation of both companies in the Act of 1839.

The Lords of the Admiralty first sent Captain Belcher, hydrographer, to survey. His proposals were published in the *Nautical Magazine* of 1837. One of his ideas was to construct a pier from the Mount but the recommendations of Denham were finally adopted. Improvement of the harbour and the inauguration of a Steam Navigation Service were vital to the success of the port but money troubles stunted the full fruition of the scheme. Owing to some loss of confidence, dock shares were not taken up as rapidly as was hoped. A true dock was not to come until 1877, but Peter's struggle to implement the original plan and bolster finances from his own pocket was yet again illustrative of his optimistic, enterprising Victorian spirit.

Regular steam and rail services commenced the day after the opening of the railway. In May 1841 *Fireking*, one of the finest and fastest steamers afloat, made the Fleetwood to Ardrossan run. Steamer services were operating to the Isle of Man and Belfast by 7 October. Paddle-steamers plied daily to Ulverston for the Lake District and the first *Fleetwood Chronicle*, on 11 November 1843, advertised 'Best route to Belfast and Londonderry via Fleetwood. The North Lancashire Steam Navigation Co.'s iron steamers *Prince of Wales* and *Princess Alice* . . . For Londonderry the powerful steamer *Robert Napier*.' In the ensuing years the servant appears to have ousted the master. Frederick Kemp owned the steam Navigation Co. and Peter was heavily in debt.

Aware of the needs of growing town and port, Peter wrote many letters from Rossall Hall to the Lords Commissioners seeking approval for the bonding of goods in warehouses which he proposed to erect for tobacco and all East India

Ships sailed to India carrying rock salt from this pier on the River Wyre at Preesall.

The late 'Couch' Wright sails the River Wyre in his prawner FD 112, heading for the Jubilee Pier.

A fleet of fishing smacks waiting for a favourable tide, c. 1902.

goods, besides making bonding arrangements for timber. He urged the removal of the main custom house from Poulton to Fleetwood. 'I pray your Lordships will give direction for such removal as soon as the requisite building can be erected and which I am willing to build immediately, having ordered a plot of land to be staked out for the site of the Custom House and suitable residence for the Officers.' Permission was granted. The original Custom House was finished in 1840 and still exists. It became Fleetwood Town Hall. Dr William Beattie, on his visit in 1842, commented on it and other Decimus Burton buildings, speaking lyrically of Fleetwood as 'this new Tyre.' The limits of the port were set out and on vellum, a 'Plan of the Port of Fleetwood with the legal quays and wharfs setting forth the boundaries thereof.'

Fleetwood was made a Warehousing Port by Treasury order on 30 May 1839, 'a supernumerary port' but a rider was added, 'Should the communication by the Ribble to Preston be improved My Lords will be prepared to reconsider the whole arrangements.' The 'Master of Rossall' was accused of serving his own ends rather than those of his parliamentary constituency when Preston was relegated to a creek under Fleetwood. Once again the Preston press took up the war cry by viciously attacking 'Fleetwood's darling scheme of aggrandisement' and Peter was challenged to a duel by Colonel Yorke Scarlett who backed MP Townley Parker's cries for the decision on the respective ports to be rescinded. Besides the Preston grumblings there were local complaints from John Bourne of Stalmine Hall and William Birley, flax merchant of Kirkham, who said their properties were not within parliamentary limits and should be toll-free. Did the improvements to the harbour justify the claim that Fleetwood stood on its own considerable merits and deserved the privileges granted? Captain Denham, in his sailing directions, pointed out that the River Wyre flowed in such a way as always to have a scouring effect on the riverbed so that its natural basin, the Canshe Hole, was preserved. The river narrowed where the new wharves were being constructed and flowed so swiftly here that all the silt deposits were kept in suspension and swept out to Morecambe Bay, where cross-currents from the River Lune carried the silt further, thus preventing a bar forming across the river mouth. At the entrance of Wyre was placed the first lighthouse of its kind involving 'the application of Mitchell's ingenious mooring screw in submarine foundations,' far superior to a lightship which could break free in rough conditions. Wyre pilot boats of sloop and yawl rig cruised between Formby and Haverigg Points. 'Happily for the mariner and this new Port enterprise few directions will be necessary to enable even a stranger to enter it. In thick weather you can feel your way.' The new screw-pile lighthouse arrived on the schooner *Collingue* from Belfast on 26 November 1839 and was erected within a day 2 miles offshore. That Peter met the blind engineer is evidenced by a letter written on 28 November. 'I saw the gentleman stone blind at Captain Denham's, who has built a lighthouse. It is beautiful to watch his intelligent countenance and he feels as proud of having invented what saves life as on account of its cleverness. How thankful did I feel to merciful God who when he took away one, left one eye to me.'

Mitchell used to work singing alongside his men encouraging their labours. He felt the structure of the lighthouse with his sensitive hands and it is said that, working over it, he detected a flaw which to the sighted had passed unnoticed. Together with the two stone lighthouses designed by Decimus Burton it shone forth on 1 December 1840 at the ceremony marking the opening of the Cut Channel to night traffic. The moment of unveiling must have been wonderful to the man whose money and enterprise had made it possible and also to the crowds who had gathered on the shores. As night descended Sir Peter, in company with other ladies and gentlemen, embarked in a steamer navigated by Captain Denham. The boom of cannon mingled with cheers. Rockets soared aloft but the rejoicing was short-lived. Records show that money was insufficient. Dock gates were opposed on grounds of cost. One steam dredger was lost on the way to

Pleasure boat stage. In 1840 it was used for trips to Wardleys old port on the Wyre. The Customs Watch House on the left was used before Fleetwood was built.

Fleetwood and the formation of a Tontine Co. to boost the undertaking was by no means an unqualified success. This aimed to assist the Chartered Co. for the construction of docks and warehouses but the directors expressed concern at the small number of shares subscribed for. At this point it seemed wise to unite railway and harbour with dock.

George Stephenson's report in 1839 had recommended that a quay large enough to accommodate three steam vessels be constructed and the result was a sturdy piece of Victorian engineering 600ft long, completed in 1841 and similar to the Brunswick Pier at the terminus of Blackwall railway.

While the railway was the means of supplying timber, coal, cotton, flax, butter, milk and eggs to Preston and beyond, trade with Ireland through the new port could make meat and poultry available at a cheaper rate than via Liverpool, some of whose trade Peter hoped to capture for his New Liverpool. 'Fired with the exorbitant charges at Liverpool, the merchants of Manchester have turned their eyes to Fleetwood,' printed the *Fleetwood Chronicle* on 5 October 1845. In the same year the Tidal Commissioners praised the harbour improvements, forecasting a thriving port on the evidence of S.P. Bidder, Frederick Kemp and Robert Gerrard, the latter a pilot of twenty years' experience who, knowing both Lune and Wyre, stated, 'Vessels have often to remain at anchor near the foot of Wyre before they can get up to Glasson Dock. That is never the case with Fleetwood. There is not the least difficulty in taking the harbour by day or night.' Belfast traders preferred Wyre to Preston because 'the former was at once open to the sea.'

Fleetwood's superiority to neighbouring ports was thus evident and trade did increase. New bonding warehouses three storeys high were erected at the corner of Adelaide Street and Dock Street, enlarging the original one. Vessels arrived from America, the Baltic and the West Indies bringing tobacco, sugar and spirits, and in 1846 the barque *Diogenes* arrived with a cotton cargo, it was hoped the first of many. A public dinner marked this important occasion. The toast of the evening was drunk nine times out of a bumper, followed by nine long and hearty cheers. In the same year a testimonial was presented to Henry Smith, Lloyds Agent, Admiralty Surveyor of steamers, (later Manager of the North Lancs. Steam Navigation Co.) for his untiring efforts to promote steamship traffic and advance Fleetwood's interests. The latter had reported in 1842 that despite an excellent harbour 'life was wanting . . . but now there is more work than there are hands to perform . . . What changes have we witnessed.' His untimely death in a railway accident the following June and that of Mr Anderson, harbourmaster, drowned the same year while he was directing the mooring of the steamer *Eclipse*, reflected the bad luck which throughout history has struck Fleetwood. On 5 January 1844 Preston was made an independent port and Fleetwood a creek within that port. John Laidlay, merchant, wrote 'I think there must be some

The North Euston Hotel, with Lower Lighthouse.

mistake . . . in reducing this port to a mere creek,' but the Custom House was closed; Frederick Kemp had to hand over the property of the Crown and business was conducted from the Watch House. There had also been the Embankment to consider, the wash of seas having made it unsafe. Re-routing was imperative for 'when the tide is up, it flows under the railway and covers the land right and left . . . which makes it appear terrific to a person who has never seen it before.' Viewed from the Crown, an approaching train seemed to be riding over the waves. There was also distress among the workers, increased by disquieting rumours that Sir Peter was in financial trouble, but no lack of fighting spirit. The town put on a bold face; 'May the tide of fortune flow on, rapidly will the port of Fleetwood stand forth in proud pre-eminence defying the futile attempts that have been made to throw a cloud over its many advantages and assign it to oblivion.' Thus spoke the loyal press and Henry Anderton came to the rescue with his pen, witheringly referring to Preston as 'that pitiful creek' but in spite of brave words the port lay uneasily waiting for signs of steady and lasting prosperity. John Power, Secretary, who resigned after criticism from the Preston and Wyre Undertaking, blamed all on a lack of implementing the original plan. 'Whilst that was continuing the town of Fleetwood progressed with great strides. Its success was the wonder of the north.' A meeting of the Railway Harbour and Dock Co. at the North Euston Hotel revealed the ramshackle state of their affairs: 'It will be recollected that the report presented April last was so far unsatisfactory especially . . . relating to the financial condition of the company as to induce the shareholders to pass a resolution appointing Mr Cottam to audit the accounts . . . although every facility has been offered . . . such was the confused state of the books that it was found impossible to prepare a statement for the proprietors.'

FOUR

That City of the Desert

Fleetwood, by applying the rare principle of good planning, was the first town in Lancashire to bear in mind the needs of future generations. Peter Hesketh's choice of planner and architect Decimus Burton, the great exponent of the British Classical style, was a typical gesture. Only the best expression was good enough. 'The well-known and highly talented architect has just left Rossall Hall after drawing up plans,' reported the *Preston Pilot* of 21 April 1836. Basically, Burton's layout was a radiation of wide streets using the Mount as a hub or focal point where all converged. This highlighted ancient Tup Hill,

Tup Hill, the largest sandhill where Decimus Burton placed his summerhouse, 1836.

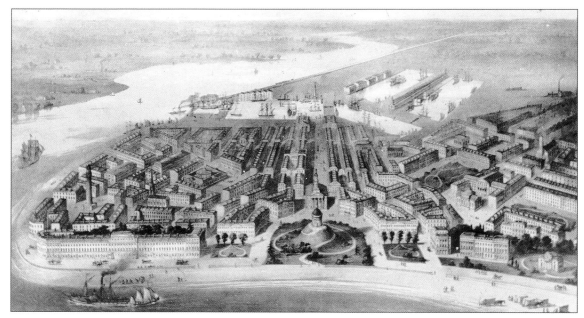

A bird's eye view used in the prospectus for the proposed 'city of the desert', Fleetwood, 1824.

time-honoured picnic spot, to be grassed and landscaped as a meeting ground and place of promenade. Important civic buildings, villas, churches and squares were indicated behind the Mount but unfortunately never built. Burton arranged for a good ploughman to mark out the lines of streets like spokes of a wheel; London Street, central and wider than the rest, to run straight as an arrow down to the docks and harbour.

P. Gauci's impression of the founder's intentions, issued with the prospectus, depicts a well-planned town of Georgian dignity viewed from on high with a thriving seaport at the rear. On this lithograph can be seen Temple View situated on top of the Mount and referred to by a visitor in 1838. The harbour, studded with sails, is graced by a tall column and several ships are sailing into port. Wide, orderly streets, neatly arranged bathing vans, horse-drawn coaches, tiny figures on horseback and the railroad vanishing into the distance of the Fylde plain, completed the idyllic picture. Both prospectus and lithograph breathe firm confidence and sincerity in this enterprise designed to express Peter's liberal ideas on how people should be encouraged to live. Copies of the prospectus were available in all principal towns of Lancashire, prospective buyers being directed to Decimus Burton's office, 6 Spring Gardens; Owen Alger's office, 37 Bedford Row; Messrs Wilson & Elletson of Poulton-le-Fylde; Frederick Kemp and the Clerk of Works at Fleetwood.

The plans were swiftly implemented. One of Owen Alger's letters reads, 'Trains filling in a surprising way, steamer takes seventy to a hundred passengers daily across to Ulverstone. The building plots are going off very fast and the houses let before they are half finished.' A month later Peter reported to Charles, 'In the buildings at Fleetwood there is from day to day, I may even say hourly, perceptible progress.' The building activity of three years is revealed in the January 1841 plan showing railway goods terminus, customs watch house, harbourmaster's office, market, gas-works, timber yards, bonded warehouse, railway passenger terminus, Terrace Walk, East Esplanade, Queen's Terrace, Bold Street, West Lane, Cop Bank and Fleetwood Place. Where buildings have arisen is clearly indicated. On Dock Street there are houses, hotels, the estate office, the bonded warehouse and streets lined with terraced houses leading to St Peter's Church. In front of the North Euston Hotel and Euston Place is an area earmarked for a statue to commemorate the founder. Sir Peter particularly admired St Leonard's and desired a similar elegance for the north-west so it was natural to choose the man who had helped in its design. Both men were founder

Mr and Mrs Lambert, who were among the first inhabitants to settle in Fleetwood-on-Wyre.

The Steamboat Pier, railway station, Queen's Terrace, Pharos lighthouse and archery ground.

members of the Athenaeum Club and met socially on other occasions such as the
Archery Contest at St Leonard's in 1835, which Peter won. To oversee progress
the famous architect occupied a house on the corner of Warren Street and Dock
Street and he also leased a house in Queen's Terrace.

By 1841 ten streets had been spread with shingle from the beach. A flow of
bricklayers, joiners, painters, plasterers, pavers and general labourers moved to
the town to find employment. Three rows of cottages were built in the Copse area
for workmen, but there was bad overcrowding, as many as sixty to a house being
reported. Captain Denham's house on the corner of Dock Street and Kemp
Street was one of the first large, private dwellings to be built. In 1845 John Walker
at a Court of Enquiry explained figures for 1840. 'There were 314 vessels which
were principally stone-laden for Fleetwood, and this was an extraordinary case,
not likely to occur again.' Development was concentrated near the river and the
railway, making Dock Street, Church Street and the area round church and
market the early town centre rather than the Mount area, a reversal of the original
intention. Sir Peter Hesketh Fleetwood's Estate Book Leases reveal this
concentration. Robert Banton of East Warren Farm laid the earliest foundation in
1836 on the south-west corner of Preston Street.

Harbour returns show that stone came from Preston, Lancaster, Barrow, Ulverston, Flint and Liverpool; paving flags from Wick. Bricks were manufactured on the Railway Co.'s land and there were brickcrofts near Flakefleet Farm and on the Rossall Estate near the Landmark, where a hoard of Roman coins was found in 1840 and taken to Rossall Hall. Thomas Parkinson, Head Carpenter for Rossall Hall, completed the Fleetwood Arms, the first hotel finished, 'offering every accommodation for visitors.' The hotels played an important part in the early days of the town serving as meeting places in the absence of a civic hall. Within their walls were made decisions affecting the whole community.

A description in a Preston newspaper from April 1841 brings the whole scene to life:

After a brisk ride by the railway, having passed along a length of flat, uninteresting country, we arrived at that portion of the line which is constructed on piles, and which may serve for a model of the projected road over Morecambe Bay. The similarity appeared more striking as the tide was flowing rapidly in, covering a tract of land (left dry at low water) which is expected in a short time to be reclaimed from the sea. It is from this part of the line that the first view of Fleetwood was presented to me, and the contrast between the dull, Dutch-looking country through which I had passed – low, level land, unenlivened by any object of interest, save here and there a distant view of a windmill, devoid of trees and intersected by broad dykes – and the handsome town to which we were hastening was very striking. The spire of the church and the lofty column of the lighthouse, towering above the numerous

The Pharos lighthouse was completed in 1840. Hundreds of early trippers climbed up the 107 stone steps for the spectacular view.

buildings with which they were surrounded, are the most prominent objects at a distance; and, as I drew nearer these masses of houses resolved themselves into rows of shops, streets, public offices, etc. On leaving the commodious station at which I had arrived, the town is seen more in detail, and conveys a curious sensation to the visitor. To my right, stretching along the quay, were numerous wharfs piled with timber, coals, slate, stone, while alongside of them were a number of vessels discharging their cargo. The entrance to the town is favourable for producing an impression of size, for a perspective view of the long line of buildings is obtained, and the upper finished parts of the streets only appears which their termination and the starr hills behind them do not show. Southwards appears the new railway hotel, with a street principally occupied by the artisans employed in the works, while opposite the railway station stretches Church Street, which appears at present to be the main resort

Mr Porter's Wyre Shipping Company vessels sailed all over the world from Port Fleetwood. Here is a throng of Sunday afternoon spectators in 1900.

More crowds on the front watching Solly's Pierrots and a magnificent paddle-steamer arriving from the Isle of Man.

of business, and occupied by different sorts of tradesmen. Walking along the beach, passing rows of good shops, public houses, dwelling houses, I came to the better part of the town; after the Fleetwood Estate Office and the bonded warehouse, I came to the Custom House, a handsome, stone-fronted building surmounted by the royal arms; opposite to which is a broad, flagged esplanade, in the centre of which a lofty flag-staff is erected. A little further on, the noise of the workmen, the sound of the hammer and the saws told of some erection in progress. A fine row of noble stone houses, superior to any in Preston, is the object of their labours and when completed they will be the handsomest terrace in the place. A balcony runs along the whole of them, and the entrance to each house consists of a fine, stone balustrade with steps. The lighthouse, a circular column on a sort of Egyptian base, stands in the opening between these houses and the new hotel. Round the lantern is a light balcony from which a fine view of the harbour is obtained. Passing this, I came to the great wonder of the place – the new hotel.

Anchors in Euston Park from centuries past. A wooden stock denotes an eighteenth-century example, and over the passage of time they have been dredged up in their hundreds.

There follows a description of the North Euston Hotel in all its magnificence epitomising the germ of the entire venture. From London Euston the nineteenth-century traveller came by rail to Fleetwood's North Euston before embarking for Scotland or Ireland the next day:

> One of the largest hotels in the north of England . . . equalled by none. In front of it stands a beautiful building like an ornamental temple, used as lighthouse . . . upon the top of which a staff with a moveable ball is fixed, used as a signal to vessels of the depth of the new channel . . . the fine bracing air which visits the Mount gives a relish to the prospect. From this elevation the whole town is seen spread out as a map, and I could perceive the sites of the intended streets staked out in every direction. The church too looks well from this spot . . . It is stated that Sir Hesketh Fleetwood intends presenting a fine organ . . . The population is very great for the size of the place. That such a place as Fleetwood should have sprung up in such an incredibly short time is a surprising proof of public spirit, that there should from absolutely nothing have started into existence a town of such beauty almost reminds one of the fables of the east. Here in a few years we have a perfect town with its Custom House, Market, Railway, Gas Works, Steam and Packet Office and every other convenience trade going on with extraordinary impulse, newcomers anxiously enquiring for shops, direct communication from Scotland and a railway straight to London.

W.G. Herdman, the Liverpool painter, prepared a set of eight beautiful lithographs illustrating the making of the town in 1839. Dedicated to the founder, sets of these were presented to Queen Victoria, the Duchess of Kent and many other notable people. Other artists' impressions appeared, Wallis's view of the Mount being best known. Day and Hague, lithographers to the queen, produced a set of engravings one of which advertised the North Euston Hotel's grand opening for May 1841, but the star attraction was not ready until August.

The enormous expenditure between 1840 and 1842 called a halt to Burton's town plan. His professional account from 1836 to 1843, amounting to £5,688 4s 2d was paid off and the famous architect went to Bournemouth on an assignment for the trustees of Sir George Tappe-Gervis. Fleetwood knew him no more but his association with Sir Peter continued right up to the latter's death in 1866.

S. Lewis's *Topographical Dictionary* of 1845 describes Fleetwood as a carefully planned town with no heritage of old buildings or cobbled streets. 'Before 1836 there was nothing but a wild tract of rabbit warren without any buildings save one solitary kiln for burning limestone. Many streets have been marked out and named but no housing development has taken place.'

Details from the Fleetwood-on-Wyre certificate book are full of interest but the haphazard items and the vague 'miscellaneous' sums tell their own story. Cottages, sea walls, hotels, Ferry House, bonded warehouse, Decimus Burton's house on Dock Street, custom house, Queen's Terrace, lighthouse, street tablets, market place, public baths, stables, tenders, plans, travelling expenses, wages – all figure if somewhat erratically, but perhaps the most human and charming item is 'the fence to Mr Vantini's yard – plank to prevent rabbits passing under gate.' Vantini was the first manager of the North Euston Hotel.

FIVE

Fleetwood Invites Us

A s the hotels and boarding houses were completed and freshly-painted shops put out their signs, in came the visitors, agog to see it all first-hand. Travellers' tales had filtered back to the sooty mill towns of Bolton, Manchester, Oldham and Wigan. Encouraged by cheap fares and day excursions, advantage was taken of a golden opportunity to view, and there is no doubt that until the novelty wore off Fleetwood had trippers in their thousands.

There had been a daily coach at Poulton during the season since 1838 to meet the Fylde Union Coach to and from the new bathing station at Fleetwood, but the railway could carry much larger numbers. The *Fleetwood Chronicle* advertised

The staff of the Fleetwood Chronicle, *one of the earliest newspapers, first printed over a stable in Dock Street, 1840s.*

The staff of the Fleetwood Chronicle *preparing to announce the death of Sir Peter Hesketh Fleetwood in 1866.*

the town as 'an unsurpassable summer residence for those seeking refreshing air in lieu of murky atmosphere and possessing advantages over every other port on the Western Coast.

If the building activity had scared the rabbits, the influx of tourists set up their general exodus. Seabirds which had from time immemorial thickly clustered the shores in such numbers that their nests could scarcely be avoided, took flight to Walney Island. Trippers plundered their nests and shell-collecting began in earnest, cutting down on the varieties for successive generations.

The beginning of Fleetwood as a resort was perhaps marked by the launching of the iron steamer *Duchess of Lancaster* in the Lune on 14 May 1840. A crowd came to Fleetwood for the day amid general rejoicing. On 21 January the same year a general holiday was declared in the town on the occasion of the launching of the first steam dredger *Success* by Mrs Denham. Crowds assembled on both sides of the river. The cannon brought from Tulketh Hall by Sir Peter and arranged at intervals along the waterfront fired a salute and inevitably a celebration dinner was held in true Victorian style.

Mona's Queen, *a paddle-steamer, off to the Isle of Man, 1890. At this time a row of cannon lined Fleetwood's waterfront.*

Lists show that distinguished visitors stayed at the North Euston Hotel; the Countess of Athlone, Lord and Lady Hamilton Chichester, the Honourable C. Marshall, Lord and Lady Monteagle, the Earl of Gosford and daughters, Lady Leichmere, Colonel and Lady Verner, Major Marsland and others.

In the passenger list to and from Belfast by steamer were Lord Beresford, Lord and Lady Seymour, the Duke of Manchester, Lord Hillsborough, Lady Berkeley, The 1850s even saw the Tsar of Russia.

The hoteliers vied with each other to attract custom. James Hornby of the Fleetwood Arms made it his 'unremitting study to provide every comfort and accommodation on reasonable terms.' Zenon Vantini, fiery Corsican, experienced hotelier and one-time courtier to Napoleon, whom Peter brought up from London, 'begged respectfully to announce to the nobility and gentry' that his hotel which was 'most beautifully situate' was complete. A horse-drawn omnibus met every train and steam packet. 'There are Baths which cannot be surpassed uniting every description of bathing now in use.' Saddle horses, carriages and sailing boats could be hired. A band from the Italian Opera House played daily in the season. The cost of a sitting room or best bedroom was 3s or 4s a day. Breakfast consisted of 'tea or coffee with eggs or cold meat – two shillings; ditto with mutton chops or boiled ham – two shillings and sixpence.' The Victorians laid a good foundation before they set sail.

From the opening of the Preston and Wyre Railway visitors came pouring into Fleetwood so that passenger traffic exceeded all expectations. The town could not accommodate all the visitors who sought lodgings so it benefited the inland Fylde towns and villages. Newspapers commented that a bed was a luxury. Many slept in coaches, outhouses, on straw in stables, or across two chairs. This did not deter others from following and the traffic through Preston by rail and road was unprecedented. 'The Fleetwood and Wyre Railroad seems to have contributed largely to this influx,' said the *Bolton Free Press*. All round Britain fishing villages were turning into resorts. The hard-pressed denizens of the mills rushed like lemmings to the coast on their days off to immerse their bodies in the sea and drink large quantities of sea water. 'Physick' and 'ozone' would do a world of good, said the doctors and the non-plussed natives of the coastal hamlets, who had hitherto regarded the sea as a grudging enemy from which they snatched a meagre living, quickly adapted to the craze. Queen Victoria had her first dip at Osborne on 30 July 1847. As railways developed, visiting the seaside was no longer the preserve of the wealthy.

The elegant houses in Queen's Terrace had been expensively fitted to receive wealthier visitors for stays of three weeks to three months. Bracing air, clean wide streets, strong sunshine, firm sands and excellent bathing accommodation, yachting regattas, firework displays, gingling matches, wrestling, cricket on the Warren, pony and donkey rides, mussel gathering, steam tug boats and pleasure yachts plying hourly, provided untold pleasure for thousands of day excursionists to Fleetwood. Sea trips on the *Nile* and *Express* to Piel and Glasson Dock were run for Sunday trippers

for 1s. There were trips to Barrow, round the bay, which 'took passengers to Bardsea for Ulverston and the Lake District'. From 15 August 1840 the *James Dennistoun* sailed to Douglas, Isle of Man, each Saturday until 5 September, and the

August of 1844 saw 10,000 excursionists eager to escape the noise of machinery and the daily grind. Here was something to give meaning to Addison's belief that Sunday cleared away the rust of the whole week. 'Double journey – single fare' was extended to other days and the Railway Co. offered attractive terms to private groups such as temperance societies and mechanics' institutes. Thomas Cook, founder of the famous travel firm used special trains. He never looked back. In 1846 he arranged transport to Fleetwood and on the Ardrossan by steamer, his parties merely passing through. In the same year the biggest Sunday school trip brought 4,200. Two engines pulled the long train which was divided for fear of accidents. There were fifty-six carriages, many little more than cattle trucks with improvised seats. The August Gala had a large marquee pitched on the Archery Ground. A military band accompanied the steam boat excursions and Mr Green 'the celebrated aeronaut' was engaged to give ascents in his Nassau Balloon.

The Poor People's Annual Summer Excursion from Preston to Fleetwood was accompanied by an informative booklet;

In the first place you should remember that the tickets are not to be given to any but the poor . . . be at the station a quarter of an hour before the time . . . a band will accompany the train and the signal for starting will be its striking up. Do not attempt to leave your seats until the train is fully stopped at Fleetwood. The amusements . . . are as follows. The steamers will continue to sail during the day round the lighthouse, at two pence each commencing at twelve o'clock when you will hear the bell ring. The Baths at the North Euston Hotel will be open at 2 o'clock, one for males and the other for females, free. Buns and milk will be given out in the Market House to commence about one o'clock indicated by the going off of a ballon [*sic*]. The Dance on the lawn, weather permitting, will follow the distribution, the place will be marked out by the Charity Banner being fixed in the sand.

Bathing in the sea may commence some time before High Water . . . and persons are cautioned not to bathe too near the Promenades.

The revolutionary Screw Pile lighthouse, Wyre Light, the first of its kind.

'Glances on the Railway' in the same publication describes the route, supplying a diagram of the Screw Pile lighthouse and statistics to add to the holiday mood. The 107 stone steps of Pharos lighthouse were well worn by the crowds who climbed them for the view.

Another annual affair was the 'Females' Cheap Trip from Preston to Fleetwood', arranged by the same Preston Committee. A return ticket was ninepence.

Employers may avail themselves of this opportunity of sending down any of the sick or other hands whom they may be desirous of treating.

The Railway Co. officials had to watch out for men dressed as women on these occasions. An undated handbill of the 1940s, issued by the Lancashire and Yorkshire Railway, announces:

'Sea Bathing for the Working Classes' – on and after Sunday morning next and on each succeeding Sunday until further notice, with a view to affording the benefit of sea bathing, a train will leave for Fleetwood and Blackpool . . . persons availing themselves of these trains will be enabled to Bathe and refresh themselves in ample time to attend a Place of Worship.

The political leader, Richard Cobden, who headed the agitation against taxes on food imported into Britain (especially corn) in 1846, paid the expenses for his workpeople to visit Fleetwood. Free Trade principles had been passed in Parliament and this mammoth trip and procession was by way of celebration, In the cotton towns of Lancashire – Bamber Bridge, Leyland, Bolton, Rochdale – the jubilant workers assembled at 6 a.m. to join the specially chartered trains. One thousand three hundred of them, with newly struck Free Trade medals hanging on ribbons round their necks, arrived in Fleetwood, their banners whipped by the sea breeze. Across from the Crown Hotel they lined up, singing, chaffing the townsfolk and parading their wide streets. They were assured of welcome. It was appropriate to celebrate here because Sir Peter Hesketh Fleetwood was avowedly for Free Trade, the 1841 election having been fought on the issue. Part of the Hesketh crest was a wheatsheaf and Sir Robert Peel had presented Peter with a seal bearing the words 'You deserve a good thrashing.' The pun may have been jest or earnest, but by 1846 Sir Robert persuaded Parliament to abolish the Corn Laws, largely as a result of Cobden and Bright's Movement. Whitsuntide 1845 saw the visit of all the workpeople of Messrs Horrocks, Jackson and Co. Gala celebrations filled the wharf with train loads.

In July 1847 there were cheap excursions from West Riding to Fleetwood and Blackpool organised by the Manchester and Leeds Railway Co. 'The most humble individual may now visit such interesting parts of his own country as are celebrated for their natural beauty or historic fame . . . a large number of marquees and tents have been purchased by the company with other materials for the convenience of pleasure parties may be had on application.' When three thousand Preston schoolchildren visited Fleetwood, eleven of these marquees were 'pitched on the Warren.'

Joseph Livesey, Lancashire social reformer and temperance advocate, instructed those on the Poor People's trips not to visit the beer shops, but to buy tea. 'Persons intoxicated will not be allowed to return by the trains.' Jowett's Temperance Hotel on Dock Street was opened in June 1841, but competition from public houses was overwhelming.

An amusing story is related of an 1846 passenger train from Preston to Fleetwood which ran through a covey of partridges near Kirkham. One bird was caught in the cinder box; soon afterwards 'a savoury odour rose from the fowl.' The fireman turned the bird over to cook the other side and by the time they arrived at Poulton it was done to a turn and the railway men enjoyed a good feed on arriving in Fleetwood.

Guests at Rossall Hall had hare coursing, duck shoots, sailing, archery and hawking to choose from. 'Mind you take the best dogs for the credit of Rossall and for your own sport,' cautioned Peter in writing to Charles. 'Let Kemp arrange to see Mr Unsworth about entering my dogs and one puppy for Knowlys for the cup.' A Coursing Club was formed in November 1839 and average 'bags' were thirty hares. After a meet they would adjourn to the Fleetwood Arms Hotel and have a 'sumptuous repast consisting of every delicacy . . . excellent dessert and wines of the choicest kinds.' Peter, described as 'a liberal and hearty sportsman', was often a winner. Yet another meeting records a costly bill of fare and 'wines of the most delicious flavour' at the Crown Hotel. The meetings were held in the grounds of Rossall Hall from 10 a.m. to 3 p.m., the Fleetwood Cup being offered for the first dog. On such occasions Peter used his hunting lodge in St Stephen's Place, which is now part of Adelaide Street. The original fireplace, stained glass and cavernous vaults still exist. As money dwindled, he sold this property for £417 14s 2d on 1 March 1847 to Stephen Burridge Junior.

Peter won a number of events in his racing yacht *Swallow*. *Lancaster Rose* was another of his craft, but all eventually had to go towards the paying off of debts.

The Archer's Field at Larkham 'where the gentry of the Grange were wont to practise that old English sport' was the meeting place of the Rossall Archery Club. Peter's brother Charles attended with his daughters on 15 September 1850 when Debonnaire (the child born at the Rectory when Peter's wife, Debonnaire, lay dying) won a quiver of arrows and Emily, her sister, came third. Close to the North Euston Hotel was also the Archery Ground, now a bowling green.

Splendid balls were held in the assembly room of the North Euston Hotel and Mr Lord, Professor of Dancing, coached the ladies. Regattas drew crowds from all over Lancashire. Fleetwood Tradesmen's Regatta was 'open to all England' for sailing, rowing and sculling. Cricket was played from the early 1840s, Frederick Kemp being president of the club; Stephen Burridge Junior, Secretary. A Choral Society was formed, too.

In a field owned by Mr James Hornby there were ploughing matches. Processions were very popular, the first one being organised in 1839 by the Oddfellows. Members from the Fylde Lodges marched down Dock Street and Queen's Terrace led by a brass band. At the Mount cheers were raised for Sir Peter Hesketh Fleetwood. Traversing London Street they stopped at Captain Denham's house in Kemp Street where the captain addressed them from a window. Dinner was served at the Victoria Hotel after a service by the Revd Mr Thurtell in the first schoolroom built opposite the site of St Peter's Church. Silk banners and glittering regalia made the ceremony impressive. It was the first of many grand processions which became a feature of town life. 'The Birth of Fleetwood-on-Wyre', a poem by Uriah Umbrah, and the verses of Henry Anderton urged people to visit the health-giving resort. 'Haste, haste to our newly-formed Paradise,' exhorted Henry.

Those early years were the halcyon time, but like so many Fleetwood ventures, a worm lay in the bud. When patronage fell away Vantini could not pay his rates. The commissioners reduced these from £1,000 to £800 and the 'Fashionable Arrivals' turned to 'Lists of Visitors' by July 1845. Vantini shook the sand of Fleetwood off his heels and left to give place to 'Mrs Sharples Hotel'. The novelty of the resort had worn off, especially for the rich.

In a desperate attempt to win back dwindling crowds and extend the season, firework displays were held on the Archery Ground, bonfires were lit on the Warren and other activities took place, such as sea excursions to Blackpool, Southport, Piel Harbour. In 1846 inhabitants urged the building of a concert hall, ballroom and theatre combined ('Erection of a Public Hall £600 estimated expense'). Mr Rampling, architect, who had replaced Decimus Burton with somewhat utilitarian ideas, was poised with the plans but nothing came of the scheme beyond a small Mechanics' Institute, one room in the Fleetwood Estate Office.

The death blow to Fleetwood as a major holiday resort was struck when the branch line opened to Blackpool in 1846. Destined to become a treeless, brash, haphazard, immensely popular neighbour – the antithesis of all that was embodied in Peter's planned town – it was impossible for Fleetwood to compete. Fickle trippers trooped off to Blackpool where the bathing had always been cheaper, and in line with Fleetwood's luck, the vans with few customers and regular trundling over the shingle eventually fell to pieces.

Blackpool, 'the Brighton of the North' with its pleasure domes and miles of sands which had originally belonged to Peter, became the darling of the working classes. It had needed only the coming of the railway to develop by leaps and bounds. It flourished on land which had to be sold off in lots to speculative builders in order to defray the enormous debts incurred in the building of Fleetwood and the railway.

The carriage drive and promenade bordering the shore to the western of Mount Terrace constructed in 1845 and later extended along Abbot's Walk was pounded by seas and fell into dilapidation. Storms caused havoc in 1847 and again in 1852 when a fearful hurricane swept over. This kind of damage coupled with declining prosperity caused families to hesitate before venturing their fortunes 'until some more regular and reliable means of gaining a livelihood was offered them than the precarious patronage of uncertain visitors seduced from their old allegiance to Fleetwood.' By 1850 all hopes of reviving the town's reputation as a resort were abandoned. Peter was to write, 'Sometimes my heart sinks within me as I look forward and backward too.'

SIX

'The Just Punishments of My Own Folly'

O n 25 February 1842 Mrs Charles Hesketh wrote to her husband from Lytham, 'last night I heard strange things touching Fleetwood Railway . . . Vantini's Hotel closed! For some time the moonlight flittings numerous and every workman of every kind paid off . . . nothing whatever to be done for three years . . . a family returned to Lytham who settled at Fleetwood, literally beggared and starving.'

It was Landmann's estimate, so wide of the mark, that formed the crux of the financial impasse ushered in between 1842 and 1843. Returns for the railway were slow to appear. Poor advisers and incompetent servants had made matters worse. Hangers-on were given notice to quit and in a letter written to Charles some years later Peter revealed:

I have had no detailed accounts tendered to me by Kemp for a number of years . . . have from time to time been promised them by him but I neither have them nor can I get them, nor will he say when I may expect them. The only account he has rendered is a cash account for 1853 and 1854 which brought forward no balance on either side but claimed a balance of near £5,000 as due from me. In previous discussions no balance was even hinted at. I have no wish to proceed harshly only I cannot go on without having the account fully rendered as I have gone on for years trusting him and therefore signing and doing all on the faith of the promised accounts. It appears so simple and proper a thing to give accounts that I cannot see why Kemp hesitates.

There is reference to Kemp's statement that only he understands the books and that Owen Alger continually reminds Peter that he, Alger, will charge compound interest on the £5,000 and £2,000 mortgages.

I cannot tell you how upset I am as I couldn't believe so harsh a threat could be made by those who have made so much by me and when I am living with not even a boy servant and endeavouring to do all I can to pay off.

A close look at these bitter years shows that disillusionment set in early. 'I have learned to wish my things in order and not to build so distant castles.' Peter worried not merely on his own account but for those smaller investors – 'The only part I am anxious about is as many persons are building and laying out money in the Warren, and that should anything happen to my life, they may feel you will at least so far go on as to carry out the improvements in the town, without which their little all of outlay would be little worth.' Charles emerges as a shrewd, competent person. In answer to the flood of correspondence he writes infrequently to Peter, his very silences seeming to exude criticism, but Charles joins to urge Kemp to 'finish the accounts at once. You know I have never been an admirer of Alger and that my personal feelings and influence have always leant to you, rather than to him.' There is no evidence in the correspondence to show that an account of Kemp's stewardship was ever made, but on the Fleetwood scene he continued from strength to strength. Director of the Fylde Timber Co., first Post Master, Director of the North Lancashire Steam Navigation Co., and in later years a promoter of the Fylde Water Board. By 16 January 1857 Alger announced Sir Peter Hesketh Fleetwood's affairs out of his hands and from 1849 to 1860 Charles Hesketh and the Preston lawyer Mr Dixon attempted to sort out the financial muddle. Charles, who managed his own affairs skilfully, no doubt grew impatient with Peter whose involvements had milked the family fortunes. Peter turned desperately to Charles: 'I did nothing without you and had given you all my past accounts that you might make yourself master of my position.'

To this day no-one knows what really happened. After the great sums of money laid out, Peter planned to live quietly at Rossall Hall. Alger had worked out a statement in 1840, a copy of which was sent to Charles, based on what was initially a very rich estate, summarising the financial situation. Charles made a copy of this on 17 February and it was also seen by John Abel Smith, banker and promoter of the Tontine Co., who agreed that it was workable – ('Alger and I go with Cortazzi to Fleetwood. We have to see bankers and to take up bills. Alger has received a letter from J. Abel Smith which will fully satisfy you.') Although it had been necessary to take out a mortgage of £100,000, the banker had advised it, for annual landed income was nearly £11,000 and the value of Peter's estates £450,000. There was the Rossall Estate with Tulketh and Burn Hall, tithes, church patronages and the Meols Estate, which should have covered all contingencies arising from the model town building. Sir Peter held £75,000 worth of shares in the Preston and Wyre Railway. It has never been satisfactorily explained. The bitter fact that his wealth was insufficient had to be faced for the chaotic state of the books killed hope. 'Each week is a pecuniary loss,' he wrote to Charles.

In 1841 his Blackpool property was sold to Mr Clifton. Mr C. Scarisbrick offered to buy Meols Hall but the family was anxious to retain it. Alger hoped to persuade Scarisbrick to take the railway shares, thus giving a good chance of success to the line which was vital to Fleetwood, but Charles, who wanted Meols, wished for no connection with the railway. He made an offer higher than that of Scarisbrick and, backed by their Aunt Hesketh from Tulketh Hall who naturally favoured Charles as purchaser, the sale was completed in 1842 for £148,000. Writing to his wife, Charles states on 7 April, 'I am thankful to say that the business is all completed and you are now squiress of Meols.'

But the everlasting drain of resources continued. Heavy interest had to be met. In a letter written almost twenty years later, Peter refers to 'the shackled state in which my affairs seem doomed to be in my own life.'

Realisation came that his possessions at Rossall Hall too must go. 'You will be glad to hear that I hope to put all my affairs right by the sale of Rossall.' From the Athenaeum Club on 25 April 1843, 'My plate will now be sold. I sell all except a few crested things. These are my very beautiful Epernes Dish Covers, with the Wheatsheaf as handle, large and small Bold Hesketh waiters, salt cellars.'

Debonnaire's double-link pearl necklace and the diamonds went in trust. A magnificent piece of plate presented in the 1840s by 300 subscribers in Fleetwood is reluctantly referred to. Peter wrote to Charles, 'I wish you would take them. They remain now not in my hands but as security for £1,000 as I pay now high interest of 10% in my different arrangements to pay off debts. I loathe to sacrifice them especially the Cup given me at Fleetwood. I do not like to sacrifice the diamonds considered so valuable when Debonnaire had them – and now not to fetch £300 . . . If I could at least for a time save these I would be very glad and you could keep them as security for a time. They could go at last if all things go downward with me.' His 'different arrangements' led him deeper and deeper into the mire and one is amazed at how little he was given in return in his dealings with Pagden, Wormald, Styan, Shepherd, Parkin, Legge – how impossible it was as securities dwindled to keep up with their rates of interest.

The sale of the contents of Rossall Hall in 1844 lasted two weeks and special trains were run on the railway which had cost such sacrifice. The two-volume sale catalogue gives some idea of the rich contents, treasures amassed over generations. Outstanding single items like the Piranesi engravings would nowadays realise a fortune. The hall was leased to the Northern Church of England School with option to purchase within seven years. Sir Peter and the second Lady Fleetwood, Virginie Marie, daughter of Señor Pedro Garcia, whom he had married in 1837, travelled south to Hill House with Louis their son. This refuge came to him through Debonnaire, but it was not to be afforded for long. He wrote from here, 'Our house is still bed-less; indeed I keep no servants. The wind comes in everywhere. Some of the thousands I have spent or given in earlier life would come in now, well.' Ill health, remorse, poverty and hounding drove the Fleetwoods to the continent. Among the enquirers for the letting of Hill House, Peter describes one couple wistfully. 'The father of the Belgian Minister's wife rolls in money.'

On 19 January 1857 he asked Charles, 'What do you think of our occupying during Louis' term time an empty house in Fleetwood, merely putting in furniture for a couple of bedrooms and a sitting room? Wherever we are we shall have no other servant but Mrs Hornby or vehicles of any sort, so that if we have a house rent free, it is only what we eat that we need spend.' But after 1844 his visits to Fleetwood were rare.

Perhaps the leaving of Rossall was lessened because of memories. As early as 1838 he had written, 'I cannot if I confess the truth yet live at Rossall. I never yet feel it now as home.' While he was abroad Peter feared for the family pictures left at Hill House lest the tenant did not take sufficient care of them. Illness and worry were never to leave him although he appears to have accepted all without bitterness. His correspondence to Charles from Italy is full of lively observation on people and conditions but deep-seated sadness and disappointment are apparent. He longs for his own country, for contentment, his own religion and a quiet mind.

In 1847 the Testimonial Schools were opened in his honour in preference to erecting a statue. In his speech he said sorrowfully, 'I have been brought up a country gentleman, unused to such undertakings as Railways.' In that same month he greeted his queen. Her visit to Fleetwood 'the youngest town and port in all Your Majesty's Dominions' was significant. Sir Peter was well-known to Queen Victoria. He had written a poem about a bunch of violets which she had sent to him. His translation of Victor Hugo's *Last Days of a Condemned Man*, together with his own *Observations on Capital Punishment*, written at Rossall Hall, was dedicated to her. When she visited Fleetwood, the quill pen with which she signed her name and the gloves she was wearing were presented to Peter and are preserved today at Meols Hall.

> I do not speak of my large debts and sales at Rossall. I have learned to view these as the just punishments of my own folly . . . I can my self see so little of what the future may be, until I have got quit of the weight of debts and anxieties that oppress my mind.

He was never to be free from either. Continually he searched heart and mind pondering the disappointments and failures.

Peter's harsh self-criticism – 'the just punishments of my own folly' should be offset by the shining success from 1840 to the present day of Fleetwood's market,

which he opened. Pictured (left) are the original market bells, used to open and close proceedings on market days. They were rung by the town crier (generations of the Whiteside family, who lived in Dock Street).

Back in England in March 1864 he wrote to Charles, 'I have taken no wine for months. I had a very serious fall at Decimus Burton's last week, rolling down all his stairs but D.V. I received no injuries beyond the shake.' This is only one of the tumbles he refers to. Possibly the loss of an eye made him accident prone. The old complaints Erysipelas and Purpura became coupled with dropsy (shortly before death he weighed 22st, avid attempts to reduce his weight were fatal.) 'Health is a blessing we do not prize enough until it begins to fail' is written in one of his last letters. Money matters eased a little in the latter years but three years before his death, the collapse of Rossall sea fences meant more good money after bad.

The oldest existing photograph of Fleetwood Market, 1853.

He had moved in 1860 to 34 Adelaide Crescent, Brighton, 'a convert to the blessings of the mind. From all the troubles I have had and the disappointments as to speculations at Fleetwood I like a very quiet life.'

The wrangling with the Fleetwood Commissioners over the Mortgage Deed and money payable by them to Sir Peter were so protracted that news of settlement arrived when he was unconscious and dying. He had at the end expressed a deep desire to see Charles, but it was too late.

His son Louis, ordained by the Archbishop of Canterbury in 1862, was described as 'full of his duties and, sincere in his avocation.' At Peter's death creditors closed in like vultures. The Fleetwood Estate Papers reveal that eight years later 'the said Sir Peter Louis Hesketh Fleetwood was on the seventh day of July last adjudicated bankrupt by the County Court of Surrey.' Louis died unmarried in the south of France in 1880 away from relations and with his death the baronetcy lapsed.

Lady Fleetwood, who according to her husband was 'reduced to a skeleton' by the privation and worry and the giving up of what little they had to educate Louis, amazingly lived on to a great age until 1900. With her were two faithful Rossall servants, Mrs Hornby and Mrs Wicks. The three ladies lived frugally for nearly thirty years by selling off small items saved from Rossall Hall. Eventually a great-nephew traced where she was living at Haywards Heath, the small dwelling stacked from floor to ceiling with 'the wreck of Rossall.' Thomas Knowlys Parr took her back to Wymering Manor and the treasures were finally willed back to their county of origin after an absence of ninety-five years.

Members of the family were haunted by fears of fresh debts and the remainder of the property with the manorial rights was bought by the Fleetwood Estate Co. in 1876, taking Rossall into another phase of history.

SEVEN

A Man of High Resolve

Peter's heartfelt cry, 'I trust all I have gone through may not be thrown away' and the mystery surrounding the collapse of his bold plans raise the question 'What then, went wrong?' This chapter strives briefly to evaluate the man and his contribution, to bring out something of his character and to reveal him as a remarkable man not merely against the background of his own age.

At 'a very numerous meeting of the inhabitants of Fleetwood and the vicinity' held at the Crown the erection of a statue in honour of Sir Peter was discussed, but fittingly his monument became the Testimonial Schools. John Lennon, Preston weaver-poet, believed him possessed of 'true charity, a gift supreme' and there are many examples of his practical sympathy towards the oppressed. Lennon's long poem was dedicated to the founder of Fleetwood, who within a few years experienced tragedy, the wrecking of hopes and the loss of a fortune, yet his spirit and pride were apparently unbroken, the suffering mind devoid of bitterness – 'Thank God I have no feeling of ill-will or anger. I judge not others and feel – that in discharging my own duties and searching my own conduct I have enough and more to occupy me.'

That he was handsome is evident from the marble bust by Thomas Smith and the portraits at Meols Hall. Sir William Ross's miniature shows Peter as a Byronic Oxford undergraduate. Margaret Carpenter's huge canvas pictures him seated, amazingly long-limbed, with daughter Anna Maria by his side (see page 8). Despite sickness and worry he remained tall and powerful. Of an accident he had in 1855 he tells Charles, 'I fell heavily on my ribs. The doctor set my arm in about three hours. They could not do it in the common way three men could not so spring my strong muscles.' Both Charles and T.J. Knowlys spoke of his endurance, unselfishness and courage during the afflictions of 1833.

The twenty-first century may set down summarily the attempt of one man to build a town as the notion of an impractical dreamer. Aided by hindsight, it may be said that the scheme was bound to fail, yet the site was good, the excellent harbour presented by nature, and the time for development was ripe. The claims of the prospectus bear investigation. Rather it was a succession of unlucky

The amazingly long pebble wall (the stones were brought from the shore) and the grassy Mount, a favourite playground for trippers and townsfolk alike.

occurrences that were in part responsible. His high ideals and misplaced trust in men of vested and narrower interests, his having to contend with the sea in building a coastal town – these could account for the failure of his plan, but to build a railway 'Magna Carta of the poorman's motive freedom' was the intelligent beginning. On his own admission however, he was unused to such undertakings and was not equipped with the necessary business tactics. Charles's annoyance is understandable for Peter was generous to a fault. One loan was 'without security but promised to be repaid out of a sum of £3,000 . . . he seems quite to forget and what was the exact sum lent I do not remember.'

He believed in sparing no expense to obtain the best even down to the firm of lithographers, Day and Hague, who served the queen. Decimus Burton, Landmann, Locke, the Stephensons, Cubitt, Denham, were names to conjure with at the top of their professions and therefore expensive to commission. Lesser lights proved even more expensive, being incapable, but the good intentions and determination of the founder can never be questioned. The old part of Fleetwood has a distinction lacking in other Lancashire towns.

The wide street planning of Burton's plan is shown here in London Street's early days.

The courage, initiative and enterprise displayed should not be overshadowed by time or explained away by wealth. Without his indomitable spirit the plans could never have gone forward. He bore all manner of setbacks – grief, criticism, adversity – with rare determination.

It would appear that he passionately cared about people and conditions rather than money. He viewed wealth in a different light from the businessman, rather taking it for granted, unaware that he was placing himself and his family in jeopardy. His words and actions bespeak philanthropic motives yet he seemed unaware that people were lining their pockets.

He distributed bedding, clothing and food to the poor tenants of Rossall and North Meols. When agitation for the repeal of the Corn Laws was shaking Parliament, he was wholeheartedly for abolition and reform. Unfailingly kind, generous and concerned for his family and relations, he gave land for churches, including Dissenters' Chapels – 'Monopolies and slavery I altogether disapprove of . . . my opinions are founded on honesty and sincerity' – for a cause in which he believed he would tire himself out. As High Sheriff he had seen harsh sentences passed at Lancaster and the question of capital punishment much occupied his mind. 'Would not the effects resulting from education be the best preventative of crime?' He appealed for a widely spread system of enlightened education and chances for honest employment. To relieve the poverty of mind and body were enlightened thoughts indeed, ahead of his time and shared by comparatively few. In such a man there seems little self-gain.

It is difficult to believe that skulduggery and misapplication of funds played no part. Fair game in his open-handedness and goodness of heart, he attracted flatterers and hangers-on like wasps to honey and appears to have been fooled. 'I have adopted so systematic a mode of expenditure that whether I was absent or present, the works will run their course, the new world of Fleetwood revolve on its axis unimpeded.' So he thought.

The Fleetwoods and Heskeths had many warnings of the sea's destructive power and it may be argued that to ignore these was foolhardy. 'I have suffered very severely from the late storms,' wrote Fleetwood Hesketh in 1814. It was a

Sir Peter encouraged fishermen from the Southport area. He built cottages for them in Upper Dock Street and Flag Street. An early fishing boat, the Sceptre *of the Clifton Fishing Company, is seen here.*

The men who built the docks that Sir Peter strove for but never saw.

centuries-long drain on the family exchequer. To keep the sea out of the town was an enormous undertaking and Peter knew of this danger, but a strong sea wall, the boast of its contrivers and considered impregnable, was thought to be the answer. Unfortunately, far less was then known about running sands and sediments. Despite the strength of sandstone blocks the sea had its way. Nature seemed to have designed the site for port and holiday resort.

Edward Baines's Directory for 1825 quoted Wyre's safety; 'It is much to be regretted that more use is not made of so advantageous a station.' Peter, a patriot, believed that trade was the lifeblood of the nation's economy and that maritime resources should be developed. Who was to know that America's Civil War would stifle the cotton trade, that rich people would not settle in the town and poor would forsake it? There is irony in almost every fact. Did he 'fail' by desiring an integrated community controlled by the inhabitants rather than the usual privileged few? His liberal principles were evidenced by the constitution of the new town, a true democracy, but few attending the meeting availed themselves of the opportunity for representation. That it proved so must have added to Peter's disappointment. In spite of his brave efforts and backing, Fleetwood was a starveling in comparison with the flourishing southern resorts close to London. He had wealthy, influential contacts but that necessary concentration did not exist in the north-west. However, the prospectus of the Tontine Co. painted a convincing picture of the natural and local advantages of the town of Fleetwood and its proximity to an area 'swarming with wealthy as well as industrious inhabitants increasing in a ratio unknown in the South of England.'

Businessmen lost confidence in a floundering project and the new town on the peninsula was not a nodal point. Its projected usefulness in serving Scotland by sea withered when the railway was routed over Shap Fell, an unforeseen event. Repeatedly the recipe for success was struck by ill-luck.

Peter's trusting nature would seem to have laid wide open the way to his manipulation, yet he was a man of the world, much travelled. He met a cross-section of people and had adventures and encounters that would go into the making of his character. His descriptive writing reveals sensibility and humour. Travelling in the Alps, he wrote thus to Charles, 'It was very cold the morning we started from the foot at the other side and before we reached the summit a regular snow storm came on. It was most wild. The carriage was above the axles in snow, one horse fell choking . . . our faces looked blue. There were long strings of mules unable to draw the wagons forward who stopped at the turns on the hills. The long ranges of dead houses half covered with snow, the desolate appearance of

Steam trawler Doris *FD 141 with fishing smacks in the background (a punt alongside) in Lune Deeps, 1910.*

earth and air and the number of houses marked as places of refuge . . . There was just enough of dreariness to excite and therefore please me but no real danger and we came down the Italian side for 24 miles.'

Reading his letters is an experience, for he writes with such immediacy and candour as the thoughts proliferate. They reveal the workings of his mind – his humour, generosity, unselfishness, his need for love and the fact that he was obsessed with the shortness of life. Apart from some which on account of weariness he himself terms 'shabby' his style is gifted, vital and given up to deep questioning especially following the break-up of his plans. Such introspection could have been a handicap in the world of business, but he was more concerned with the fate of his soul and those in his care than in material possessions. Had he wished, Sir Peter Hesketh Fleetwood could have turned his back on the world's suffering, but he was aware of it wherever he went, on his own estates, in his constituency, in Naples and in Galway where he was carried on the shoulders of the people in a crowd of 20,000.

He made a remarkably brave and bold attempt, laying the foundations for those who followed, enabling a community to grow all the more vigorous because it was born of striving. Financial crashes were frequent in Victorian times but he and his courageous wife emerge like thoroughbreds with none of the usual attendant sordidness. Any squalor hangs round the little men of the money game. Admiration increases when it is considered how, at a stroke from such lavish sense of occasion as the High Sheriff ceremonial he had to ponder over a penny stamp and cope with draughty Hill House where he had neither a spoon nor fork, yet adapt he did. In Naples he sallied forth in a straw hat, basket on arm, to barter for fish, bread, melons – and to observe poverty.

By dint of self-denial the debts were paid and contrary to popular belief it needs firmly stating that Sir Peter Hesketh Fleetwood was never a declared bankrupt.

EIGHT

The Fleetwood Commissioners to Sir Peter Hesketh Fleetwood

The Fleetwood Improvement Act which received Royal assent on 18 June 1842 and contained 310 clauses was a landmark in the town's history '. . . for paving, lighting, cleansing, watching and otherwise improving the Town of Fleetwood.' The expenses of its passage through parliament were met by Peter five years before he retired from politics and until the management passed into the hands of the townspeople he levied his own rate. Thereafter the local authority could authorise rates or assessments not exceeding 2s 6d in the pound in any one year.

At the first general meeting held at the North Euston Hotel, the first duty of the Commissioners was 'to ascertain and settle the amount due to the said Sir Peter Hesketh Fleetwood.' Every male resident aged twenty-one years and over, provided he was not a bankrupt, was eligible for appointment as Commissioner. Committees ran for a six months term but could be re-elected; the offices of Clerk and Treasurer to be kept entirely separate. Proof that officers entrusted with money had to give security is shown in the Minutes Book for 22 August 1842 where it states, 'ordered that the salary of Mr Edmundson the collector be three pence in the £ on the amount of rate collected and that he do give a bond for the due fulfilment of his office in the amount of £200.' The district legally assigned to St Peter's Church defined the limits of the Act and the numerous clauses cover many headings – sewers, drains, paving, buildings, rubbish collection, street cleansing, lighting, fire fighting etc., in all cases safeguarding the rights of the Duchy of Lancaster and the Lord of the Manor. 40s penalties for offences against the Act are listed in detail. In keeping with its splendid beginning it is obvious that Peter wanted his town to be clean, orderly and safe with a high moral tone. No houses could be thatched and any existing thatch had straight away to be

Fleetwood's police force.

replaced with non-combustible materials. On suspicion of canine madness dogs were to be confiscated and subsequently destroyed. Stray cattle and horses were taken by the police constable to the common pound which is shown on the first Ordnance Survey map as being near the gas works. Riding or driving cattle and horses had to be done with care. No rugs, carpets or mats were to be shaken before 8 o'clock in the morning and further listed as punishable offences are indecent exposure, displaying profane books, blowing horns or noisy instruments, throwing stones, flying kites, playing games in the street, making slides in icy weather, burning rags, setting fire to chimneys or keeping swine.

A study of the minutes together with the surveyor's accounts gives a clear picture of the making of the main streets and their drainage. The town begins to take shape in the mind's eye peopled with the men who directed operations and tightly held the purse strings. These records show that stripped of the baronet's munificence Fleetwood was pitifully hard up, every job being done with stringent frugality. Severe censure was heaped upon the wretched gas-fitter who dared to repair a lamp without permission, although the amount written in faded brown ink appears to be only 1s 9d. Reading the beautiful copperplate penmanship of the minutes throws to light economic details which are in stark contrast to the baronet's generous style.

Unless the greatest care was taken over drainage they foresaw heavy expenditure. This was a problem down the years owing to the nature and lie of the land, so heavy penalties were levied on people who caused drains to be blocked. Mr Foster called 'the attention of the meeting to the state of the public sewers. Several neighbours were complaining about them, particularly those near Warren and Church Street which were in a very dirty state.' The back street between Church Street and Cottage Court was disgraceful – 'cesspools overflowing.'

The committee, reporting on drainage problems on 5 October, consisted of the ubiquitous F. Kemp, J. Leidley, K. Smith and D. Elletson, assisted by R.B. Rampling and D.D. Neve, Surveyor, and on 9 October the Drainage and Sewerage Committee drew up specifications for forming drains.

The New Market opening in November 1840 in the presence of Sir Peter and his second wife, was reported in the *Preston Chronicle*. It was to prove one of the great features of the town and is famous to this day. Wheat, meal, potatoes, apples, pigs, vegetables, flour, geese, hens, eggs, jams, pickles, and a harvest of local prawns, shrimps, crabs and inshore fish, together with farm-baked bannocks and pies were all on display together. The commissioners decided on market days,

follows, viz. :--

"And be it Enacted, That no person shall hawk, sell or expose to sale in any place within the limits of this Act, except in the present market or in such additional market-place, or his own dwelling-house or shop, any provisions or other goods or commodities mentioned in the Schedule (E.) to this Act; and any person who shall, after the opening of such market, hawk, sell or expose to sale any of the articles aforesaid in any place within the limits of this Act except in the markets of the said Sir Peter Hesketh Fleetwood, his heirs and assigns, or his own dwelling-house or shop, shall for every offence be liable to a penalty not exceeding Forty shillings."

NOTICE IS HEREBY GIVEN,

That any person or persons hereafter offending against the said Section, will be proceeded against as the Law directs.

J. M. JAMESON, C.E.,

A clause from the Fleetwood Improvement Act relating to market trading. The market has been a continuing success since 1840. J.M. Jameson was Sir Peter's civil engineer.

but tolls and dues were regulated by the Lord of the Manor. Provisions also came on the Irish boats – firkins of lard, bundles of yarn, butter, cheese, cattle. In 1844 'Her Majesty' was reported battling through gales with supplies from Ardrossan. Prices were settled by the farmers and dealers who met in the market room of the nearby Victoria Hotel. In those early days salmon was only 10*d* a pound, lobsters 1*s*, 16 eggs 1*s*, butter 6*d* per pound and oats 3*s* 10*d* a bushel.

In 1841 there were three constables and one sergeant at 1 Flag Street, the first police station, but the force was later cut to one man who appears to have had rather too much to do! The first persons to be fined under the Act were James McEllin and Ann Bell for wheeling barrows on the footpaths, but magistrates G. Thornber and U. Birley let them off on payment of costs (6*s* 3*d* each) and a promise of good behaviour. The pollution of streams entailed a fine of £200, a far-sighted piece of legislation, and the Lancashire saying 'sweep before your own door' could have originated in Fleetwood for this was the first Improvement Act in the Fylde. Failure to sweep the pavements in front of houses before 10 o'clock rendered tenants liable to a fine of 5*s* for each offence. The upkeep and cleanliness of the streets was praised at a time when this was not general. Poulton's streets were appallingly muddy and Kirkham was known to have 'heaps of manure' and 'piles of stinking offal from the slaughter houses' lying in back yards. Similar obnoxious habits were reported from Lancaster 'where no care appears to have been taken of the streets which were in a deplorable condition' although the town was prosperous.

In 1854 a row of modern cottages in Poulton Road and a police station in West Street were built, part of an effort to give a more finished appearance to the town, for little building had been undertaken since the first magnificent spurt. The partial drainage scheme was also continued. For the first fifty years the population depended on wells for its water supply and many of these are still to be found in the cellars of those houses situated in the old part of the town. One still in use in 1973 in the Town's Yard, London Street, was adapted to feed standpipes in the streets where the water cart filled up for dust-spraying or swilling the abattoir. These wells, some of which have been covered with strong wood sleepers and paved over, are all plotted on the first Ordnance Survey map.

Dr R.A. Ramsey and J.J. Elletson, surgeon, stressed the importance of good drainage for health. Cesspools, common all over the country, bred disease. Although Fleetwood had some serious outbreaks of scarlet fever, it was free from cholera, possibly because of its remote position on the peninsula. Danger to Fleetwood's inhabitants lay in seepage from the cesspools contaminating the drinking water owing to the sandy, porous nature of the soil. Not until 1890 was drinking water available from the Fylde waterworks.

Attendances at commissioners' meetings were poor, which held up progress, for without the quorum of five no business could be done. Officials, often part-time, were paid poor wages, for example a clerk received £15 per annum, a surveyor £10. Collectors frequently threatened to resign and complained of the barrage of bad language they received from householders, for collecting the rates was no easy task. Some of the meetings were held at awkward times for working men, which may have explained absences, but lack of interest was a contributory factor. Members were drawn from the middle-classes – surveyor, solicitor, chemist, civil engineer, innkeeper, tailor, merchant, printer, builder. Names of Commissioners and leading men involved in the town's business in the early years include Thomas Drummond, George Laurie, Joseph Walmsley, William Porter, Samuel Bidder, Andrew Synett, Edmund Forrest, H. Bazett Jones, Edward Edmundson, A. Buchanan, J. Goslin, John May Jameson, Joseph Bissett and Richard Ball. A fresh valuation of all the property in the district was ordered in 1843 when Mr Neve, Mr Haythornthwaite, miller, and Mr James Whinney, farmer of Burn Hall, made the valuation ('one guinea to each man for loss of time and trouble'). Alteration of the bridge leading to Rossall was ordered 'with as little expense as possible' and the surveyor procured a water cart when he attended the sale at Rossall Hall. An old manual engine from the same source served as the first fire-fighting equipment. The numbering of houses and properties (it was reported) in 1845 was carried out 'in the most economic manner.' Listed on a pathetic single sheet, expenditure for 1845 was as follows:

The group of Fleetwood Commissioners assembled when the docks were planned in the 1860s. The contractors' engine Fleetwood *is shown, in which Sir Peter had travelled in the first trip of the Preston and Wyre Railway more then twenty years earlier.*

To cost of roads outside the town	£32 11s 6½d
To cost of roads inside the town	£103 5s 3d
Materials	3s 3d
Glazing lamps	£2 10s 4d
Implements	£1 16s 10d
Whole expense from 1 Jan. – 31 Dec. 1845	£140 7s 2½d

The purchase of two birch besoms and one new paving hammer seems to be an event! Work on channelling, slutching, cleaning cesspools, gravelling, stone-breaking, getting up cinders and spreading marl is reported steadily. Sand blowing from the beach and banking in front of the North Euston Hotel gave trouble and the committee considered the cost of covering the road with marl brought by pontoon (£8 10s 6d) but they were ordered to consider a cheaper plan.

Prudence and foresight to save expense mark the conduct of the commissioners. One report advises waiting to observe the effect of weather on marl from the Knot and if this proved unsatisfactory to change to slutch from Cold Dubbs. Even nature, though not cooperative over sand, had to work for her living. Gravel from the beach was collected in quantities and stored for future use in the Town's Yard.

A gas company was formed in Fleetwood on 8 October 1840, William Strode being manager, Charles Woodbine foreman, William Woodbine labourer (wages 15s per week) and Abel Woodbine, labourer's boy (4s per week). The shareholders included Sir Peter, Owen Alger, Decimus Burton. At a meeting in 1845 at the Crown Hotel, after much deliberation 'being of the opinion that no lamp could be removed to the corner of Warren Street the Commissioners considered the only plan in the circumstances was to place an additional lamp there for three months, Mr W. Porter agreeing to light it for the sum of £1.'

The Mortgage Deed labelled 'The Fleetwood Commissioners to Sir P. Hesketh Fleetwood Bart., 13th December 1842,' proved a bone of contention for years. After the baronet's lavish provision his treatment by the commissioners seems shabby, but according to their lights they doubtless thought it necessary to get rid of the millstone by whatever means they could. At the first meeting after the passing of the Act, twenty-eight members gathered at the North Euston Hotel and all agreed that the sum of £11,816 9s 1d was due. Elletson, Jameson and Haythornthwaite were 'empowered to execute the mortgage deed' but 'the Commissioners not being at present provided with a sufficient sum to enable them to pay are desirous of securing the same to Sir Peter Hesketh Fleetwood together with interest thereon.' The sum, full details of which are on record, was to be repaid out of the rates. It was a very modest figure compared with the founder's full outlay. No charges are included for the lighthouse, hotels, or buildings.

There was much petty squabbling among the commissioners. A new Mortgage Deed appears to have been drawn up in 1861, the proceedings as reported by the press being most confused, and Mr Noblett, Chairman, was unable to keep any kind of order. Having decided to adopt the Poor Rate as a future basis for their assessment in repayments, they argued, consulted Counsel in Manchester, found all manner of loopholes, would not pay Mr Noblett's expenses and indeed threatened legal proceedings against this gentleman 'unless he deliver to the Commissioners' Clerk the Counsel's opinion on the subject of the amount payable to Sir Peter Hesketh Fleetwood.' Mr Noblett was obviously holding cut for his expenses (£5 7s 6d)!

On 4 April 1864 the commissioners, threatened with a Mandamus order, still played for time, attempting a last stand to avoid extraction from them of the full amount due, although they feared that verdict would go against them. An unexpected advantage turned up when Sir Peter could not do without the money any longer and signified through his lawyer, Harry Styan, willingness to accept their figure. The Commissioners, however, wanted a receipt that would free them from all further claims – to which they were not entitled. A special committee wrangled from December 1865 to June 1866, meeting eleven times. Mr Fox, their lawyer, met Mr Styan at the Steamer Hotel. All claims for interest from 1861 to 1865 appear to have been written off as bad debts and the sum due to Sir Peter was fixed by Styan at £926 7d; not surprisingly the commissioners' estimate was lower (£794 9s 3d). After a long struggle a cheque for £744 8s 3d was paid to Lady Virginie Hesketh Fleetwood on 28 June; Styan, for his legal services being paid £50.

The much disputed sum was again gone into by the Fleetwood Estate Co. who purchased what remained of the land with its manorial rights. Two letters written by Harry Styan in 1888 reveal the loss of a document:

I cannot find a copy of the plan but have a strong recollection of giving it to Mr Briggs. The original deed passed under Sir Hesketh's will to Lady Fleetwood and Sir Louis and by their direction it was sold to the Law Life. I believe, however, the Commissioners raised the money by debentures and paid off the Law Life . . . In 1842 there were but ten streets in Fleetwood. It was in consequence of there being no plans and in fact no streets that the deed of 1861 was searched into . . . You may take it the Commissioners have nothing to show beyond the Deed of 1861.

The frugal, stern commissioners of 1842 may be pictured in their tall hats hurrying to evening meetings at the Crown Hotel, thankful not to be trekking over the dunes to the North Euston Hotel. Deep in thought, did they wistfully ponder on harnessing the moon instead of paying Mr Strode's account for town gas? It is

The Crown Hotel, Dock Street, where commissioners' meetings were held. Built in the 1850s it was used for balls and grand dinners and was opposite the first railway station.

on record that Billy Whiteside was ordered not to light the lamps on moonlit nights and they issued an ultimatum to the gas company, finally buying them out at a low figure with the same perspicacity as they purchased the market in later years. And so in the 1840s the baronet's town, not quite true to his dreams, presented wide streets, elegant buildings and a sounding sea with bustle during the day, especially when the market was held, but dark, quiet streets on wintry nights, which were not well lit. Beyond the clusters of houses lay acres of virgin sand with the skeleton pattern of unmade streets.

Perhaps Peter's greatest enemies were his fellow-men, the very ones for whom he had striven, but this redoubtable group from the nineteenth century pulled Fleetwood-on-Wyre up by its bootstraps at a most critical stage in its development.

Billy Whiteside, the first bellman and bill poster for the new town.

NINE

'It is no Easy Task to Protect the Community from the Sea'

'You will have heard how heavy the damage at Rossall was this Autumn, many thousand pounds to me. These are heavy drains upon a man's purse who has, one way or another, had some hard pulls on it before.' Sir Peter Hesketh Fleetwood wrote this only three years before his death. Indeed the fate of the town has been so much bound up with the sea as friend and foe, that no history could exclude its effects. Beckoning to bather and angler in summer, what of its sweeping storms whipped by gales that have claimed lives and flooded property?

The Fleetwood lifeboat has the most distinguished record of all round the Fylde coast. Established in 1859, the station served continuously apart from a temporary closure (1930–3). The Journal of the proceedings of the Lifeboat at Fleetwood has for its first entry, 'Trial trip, Wind N.W., Strong gale with heavy squalls. Volunteer crew all first time in lifeboat.' Answers to signals of distress make exciting reading and reveal the unselfish, heroic nature of men. Like scaling

Lifeboat crew (Jeff Wright centre, with carnival queen), 5 October 1941, after the Stella Marie *was wrecked. She was one of the last sailing ships on the Lancashire coast. Lifeboat coxswain Jeff Wright and mechanic Sid Hill were both awarded RNLI silver medals.*

Stella Marie *was wrecked sailing from the Faroes. A dangerous but successful lifeboat rescue was achieved by Jeff Wright and crew in 1941.*

The wreck of the Pearl, *October 1895.*

mountains and exploring unknown territory, the thrill and satisfaction of battling with the elements to save life, it seems, has an irresistible pull, divorced from safety and financial gain. The busy period of the port between 1887 and 1892 saw two lifeboats. The first lifeboat house, constructed of timber at a cost of £165, was almost completely washed away by heavy seas on 20 January 1863. Lifeboat and carriage were retrieved only with great difficulty, but a replacement building was erected in the same year and in 1879 a new wooden lifeboat house was built on poles on a fresh site. Sand drifting onto the slipway had been a problem over the years and a further change was made in 1901 when the whole building was moved lower down, the operation being financed by the Railway Company. Because of the sand problem and damage by heavy seas the 1863 housing was in a brick building opposite Pharos lighthouse, but this was probably not suitable for swift launching.

The first lifeboat, 32ft long and unnamed, operated from 1859 to 1862 and saved thirty-two lives. Necessity would be alerted by severe gales 1839–40, 1847 and the hurricane of 1852.

Lifeboat (unnamed)	1859–1862	32 lives saved
Edward Wasey	1862–1880	28 lives saved
Child of Hale I	1880–1887	24 lives saved
Child of Hale II	1887–1892	13 lives saved
Edith	1887–1894	19 lives saved
Maude Pickup	1894–1930	117 lives saved
Sir Fitzroy Clayton	1933–1935	4 lives saved
Frederick H. Pilley	1935–1939	19 lives saved
Ann Laeticia Russell	1939–1975	150 lives saved
Inshore lifeboat	1966 to present	16 lives saved
Lady of Lancashire	17 January 1975	20 lives saved

The grand totals up to January 1977 were: 363 recorded launchings and 444 lives saved.

In July 1975 the Duke of Kent arrived to name the latest lifeboat, the anonymous gift of a businessman; this craft being moored permanently in a lifeboat pen once and for all solving the problem of drifting sand.

The story of Fleetwood-born missionary Percy Mather told in *The Making of a Pioneer* evokes the lifeboat scene:

One maroon – a lifeboat practice, two – a distress call to be answered, perhaps a wreck. The town is filled with the sound of clattering feet. Everyone is making for the lifeboat house; everyone is on the run. In an amazingly short time the lifeboat house is surrounded. Some scramble onto the beach; others hang round the door, peering through the cracks . . . a distress flare is seen and in its glare the wreck shows up, a barque, helpless on Pilling sands, being battered by the billows. The crew can be seen huddled together on the poop. The lifeboat crew are pulling on their oilskins, sou'westers and cork jackets; each climbs to his place then comes the great plunge into the water. She is covered from stem to stern by a huge wave; she shakes herself like a shaggy dog. The brown sails are set and away she goes into the darkness.

Schooners, brigs, barques, sloops, smacks, brigantines and steam ships with names like *Ann Mitchell, Jane Roper, Vermont, William, Inga, Venus, Eden, Olga, Labora, Theda, Louise, Zillah, Diane* – have all had cause to be grateful. Between 1860 and 1898, 188 lives were saved. The wreck chart pinpoints areas where ships got into difficulties and the boards reveal the times of year particularly prone to gales, indicating also the advent of the steamships onto the sea lanes.

The three-masted barque Clara, *her sails torn to ribbons by gales.*

The lifeboat *Edward Wasey* was named after the brave man who gained a silver medal and three service clasps from the RNLI for rescuing seven men from the *Ann Mitchell* and the *Jane Roper*, four from the schooner *Catherine* wrecked off Fleetwood on 13 February 1860 and fifteen men and a pilot from the barque *Vermont* of Halifax, Nova Scotia, stranded in a gale. On a lighter note is an account of the *Edward Wasey* on the occasion of the opening of Fleetwood Docks when the lifeboat was launched from the quay and the crew 'accidentally' fell into the water. A popular local character, Richard Wright, nicknamed 'Dicky Darby', 'feigned to be so far gone it appeared to take the crew a considerable time to bring him round.'

Famous coxwains have included James Turner, Jim Docherday, Thomas Leadbetter, Robert Wright, David Leadbetter, Jack R. Leadbetter, and William Wright. The Leadbetters, Wrights, Wilsons, Bonds and Rimmers descended from Fleetwood's earliest residents, who as fishermen, have played heroic parts as lifeboatmen. The pattern from the earliest years shows hazardous struggles with the sea fought regardless of personal safety. Successful rescues owed much to the skill gained in their daily calling.

The full force of a terrific gale struck the Fylde coast on 28 January 1860 and strewed it with wreckage. Three men were drowned and the mail steamers could not leave port. On 28 September 1875 the Liverpool schooner *W.K. Chapman* was wrecked off Fleetwood on Shell Wharf. Between the Landmark and Rossall School much wreckage was found – the ship's bell, a linen bag and the named stern part of the vessel which rapidly went to pieces. 'The gale during the night was of a most violent character and the sea so rough it would have been impossible for a small boat to live many minutes'. Captain William Swarbrick of the steam tug *Wyre* which assisted at many rescues including the *Inga*, was one of Fleetwood's early pilots. His Pilot's Certificate and Deed of Gift willing his brass telescope and weather glass are still preserved.

John Leadbetter was one of seven brothers all connected with the sea. He never had a day's illness in his life.

The 1894 storm involving many of Fleetwood's fishing smacks (*Red Rose, Mayflower, Surprise, Petrel*) wrecked the *Abana, Skulda* and *Furo*. At certain times of the year the ribs of the *Abana* can still be seen, as can the wreck of the Faroese schooner *Stella Marie*. During this fierce storm the *Falmouth* struck Rossall Point. The bodies of all the crew, including the captain's wife and child, were later washed up, and St Anne's pier was cut in two by a trawler. A huge wave overthrew the St Anne's lifeboat 'snapping the main mast 10ins thick like a clay pipe. We might as well have pulled at the Tower as tried to use oars.' In the same great gale of December 1894 the Fylde Rubber Works in London Street was blown down.

On 16 June 1897 the *Maude Pickup* made history by rescuing seventeen men from three wrecks. The crew of the *Old Hunter* bound for Mevagissey with a cargo of coal was rescued in 1907 by the *Maude Pickup* in heavy surf. Next day the crowds went to view and the newspaperman was carried out with his heavy camera equipment on the shoulders of a sturdy Fleetwood fisherman. One of the saddest occasions was the capsizing of the St Anne's and Southport lifeboats in 1866. Three meetings were held in the Whitworth Institute and Queen Hall, Fleetwood, to raise funds for the distressed widows and children. Another sad loss is recorded on the monument in Euston Park – 'erected by public subscription to the memory of James Abram and George Greenall who lost their lives in the storm of November 1890 while heroically endeavouring to save

Shipwrecked sailors landed at Fleetwood from the wreck of Old Hunter, *1906.*

The Bourne Arms at Knott End. Sailors wrecked on Pilling Sands on the night the Utility *foundered made their way here, but the cabin boy died from exposure.*

others.' Although hazards at sea were reduced with steam power and improved craft in the twentieth century, danger remained. The Ayr Steam Shipping Co.'s steamer *Carrick* was involved in a collision near Ailsa Craig in 1906. Captain Leadbetter of Fleetwood refused to leave his ship. The *Briarlyn* made headlines in 1928 and in the same year on Christmas Day lifeboat men battled through the storm wearing their Sunday best under their oilskins. Invariably there were more volunteers than places and fourteen who left festivities got a seat in the boat. Three miles north of Wyre Light the 6,000-ton liner *Tchad* had dragged anchor and was being swept onto Pilling Sands. The crew of six, including three Fleetwood men, were on their way to Heysham where the liner was to be broken up. Once the distress flares were exhausted the skipper ordered mattresses to be burned, and guided by the flames the lifeboat men battled for two hours before they reached the exhausted men.

Mountainous seas battered the Belgian trawler *Commandant Bultinck* of Ostend, wrecked off Rossall School in 1929. The saffron-walled building from Rossall Hall known as 'the wreck barn' housed shipwrecked sailors until a branch of the British and Foreign Sailors' Society was formed; the Bethel in Kemp Street and the New Fielden Sailors' Rest (1897). The latter, built on the site of Gibson's Shipyard, became the Royal Mission for Deepsea Fishermen in 1913.

The fountain subscribed for after the death of heroic sailors Mr Abram and Mr Greenall, who were drowned. A monument was later built in their honour.

Retrieving wreckage, smuggling and possibly even wrecking in the early days went on off the Fylde coast. James Potter, parson of Pilling in 1802, a popular preacher and a lover of cockfights, would join with his congregation to rescue contraband before the customs men arrived. At Meols Hall are two blue and white Chinese vases said to have been washed ashore at Rossall and taken to Rossall Hall. To the Lord of the Manor belonged the right to wreck of the sea and this passed to the Fleetwood Estate Co. whose records show much vexation regarding flotsam and jetsam.

It is not surprising that the Rossall area known as Quaggy Meols (a combination of salt marsh and sandhills) was long neglected because of its isolation and danger from the sea's advance. The Mount itself, built up by north westerly gales, was in danger in the nineteenth century. In the *Fleetwood Chronicle* appeared a poem in 1885; 'The Lost Promenade', and D.G. Rance's report of 1875 refers to 'The Mount, which hillock is being fast worn away by the sea, the terrace walk on the seaward side having entirely disappeared.' The Commissioners were forced to take action. Ralph Porter, an old inhabitant who kept a record, graphically described the destruction of the White Houses in 1869 (site of the present Mount Hotel). Tully Bank, composed of stones, shingle, starr grass and sand, began to form in 1856, gradually extending eastwards for two miles to the Lower Lighthouse and causing tides to sweep round it with great violence. In Sir Peter's childhood arable fields and pastures had covered the area. The phenomenon of coast erosion is offset by the giving back of land. The removal of gravel and cobbles by the commissioners, the Lancashire and Yorkshire Railway and the taking away of great boulders at Rossall Point for Liverpool pavements resulted in the breakthrough of Tully Bank. As far back as 1637 coastal erosion was considered a threat. A Board of Trade Order in 1905 prohibited the removal of boulders from the shore between Blackpool and Fleetwood. It was estimated that between 1844 and 1876, 30 acres of land had been lost. The Fleetwood Estate Co. attempted to cut down erosion by erecting groynes in 1876. The north side of Fleetwood, where in the 1930s the Marine Gardens and foreshore improvements were developed, presents an example of accretion. It was on the western side of the town that the sea won hands down until adequate defences were made.

Bold Fleetwood Hesketh constructed a limestone embankment at Rossall which was hoped would be impregnable to the fiercest assaults, but the storm of 1833 swept it away. Subsequently the limestone was used in Fleetwood buildings. Sir Hesketh Fleetwood's Lancashire Estate Act of 1850 refers to Indentures of Agreements made on 2 March 1848 and 10 October 1845. The price Sir Peter paid to the Duchy of Lancaster was one-twentieth part of the actual value of the land. John May Jameson designed plans and sections for breakwaters and a great deal of time and money was spent on the problem, Sir Peter undertaking the enormous job of reconstructing the wall in 1834 following the disastrous storm. Typical of his enterprise was this clay revetment paved with stone stretching from old Angersholme, Cleveleys, to Rossall, but between

Blocks from the 1833 break-up of Sir Peter Hesketh Fleetwood's original sea wall at Rossall.

1834 and 1854 these works suffered greatly and D.G. Rance refers to the wall in 1877 as 'now entirely gone to decay, far less remaining standing than is destroyed.' It is now known that problems of running sands and saturated silts existed of which they had no idea and which only modern methods have been able to solve.

In 1927 attention focussed like a burning glass on the peninsular town of Fleetwood. After several days of wild, gusty weather a strong south west gale was blowing on the night of 28 October. The direction of the wind changed due west and increased in force about 10.30 a.m., raising the predicted height of the tide to over 33ft. By 11 p.m. it was pouring over the western boundary. The first man to know, the engineer at the pumping station, was powerless to send warning as his telephone wires had been blown down. A huge tidal wave rushed into Fleetwood and within minutes many houses in the town were flooded to a depth of 7ft. The miracle was that it happened at night when most people were in bed. Next day Fleetwood hit national headlines in gale-swept Britain. 'There have been amazing flood scenes in Fleetwood. The town is isolated following a tidal wave. Four caravan dwellers have lost their lives. Beds have been put up in schools and cinemas and last night police and volunteers working in boats with flares were rescuing drenched residents. Sea walls and Promenades have been smashed by mountainous waves.'

About 150 million gallons of water had to be disposed of. At high tide there was no drainage at all. The *Blackpool Gazette and Herald* reported 'to release the water . . . three sluices have been cut in the Copse so that the vast lake extending from the engine sheds at Fleetwood to the Salt Works at Burn Naze may 'be drained into Copse Brook, the natural water course which empties itself into the harbour near Wyre Dock. . . . This has been the blackest day in Fleetwood's history. The homes of over 1,200 families have suffered incalculable damage.'

From Saturday morning until Tuesday noon the town was completely cut off. Families were marooned in dwellings to a depth from 3–10ft until rescue parties in boats went to their relief. Not until Wednesday morning was there electric light. A Relief Fund was set up by the Mayor of Fleetwood, Charles Saer.

'No less then £100,000 is needed.' Donations came from all over the country. Queen Mary and the Prince of Wales sent £50 each; 230 tons of coal was donated by two colliery firms in Wigan; 1,003 loaves from Messrs Hovis, tons of clothing and blankets, jam from Lord Derby, 25 gallons of carbolic acid and 2cwt of disinfecting powder from Calverts of Bradford. The 'Leeds Convoy' lorries, laden with supplies, rolled up to cheers and tears as to a beleaguered garrison.

Two thousand tons of timber logs from Keay's Saw Mills had floated in all directions to end up in the strangest places. Lord Street was littered with them. Pigs and cattle were drowned. Furniture in lower rooms bumped against ceilings and burst doorframes. Some houses still bear the salt-marked flood level. The tidal wave is recalled by many people as sounding 'like the roar of a lion.' When the waters subsided a sticky, black mud covered everything and 100,000 tons of refuse was carted away. Parties of boys and masters from Rossall School, Sir Peter's old domain, came to the rescue in boats and never was Fleetwood's indomitable spirit put more to the test.

On 29 July 1927 the Fleetwood Urban District Council Act had received Royal Assent, giving powers to construct and maintain adequate sea defences. The first 1,900yds was completed in 1930 and opened by the Earl of Derby on 22 April.

One of the many inundations and one which affected Sir Peter most adversely was 'the meeting of opposing seas' on 30 December 1833, which destroyed a

Described as 'a friend for all seasons' and 'a child of the seas' it is interesting to know that the Lofthouse Company raised 50 per cent of the cost of a relief lifeboat for the RNLI to provide cover for those out of service. Doreen Lofthouse and her husband are seen here alongside the mayor and mayoress of Wyre, 1993. A valuable service has been offered in the form of free charts for fishermen showing the location of submarine cables. Without these aids, supplied by Fisherman's Friend, unsuspecting vessels could capsize by catching fishing gear on invisible hazards.

portion of the coast road on the Cleveleys side, swept into the park of Rossall Hall, defying the cobbled enclosing wall. Cattle, deer, rabbits and hares were drowned, vines in hothouses ruined, outbuildings and paddocks swept away. The boathouse where Peter's yacht *Swallow* was kept filled to such an extent that when next the doors were opened the yacht launched herself. The cottage at Fenny had water washing its walls and coming down the chimney, sweeping furniture out of doors, the inhabitants fleeing in terror. Following the moving back of Fenny four times, it was finally abandoned. This same storm battered and wrecked eleven ships at sea, damaged farms, blew down Preesall windmill and undermined the Landmark. Fleetwood's history can well be described as storm-tossed!

TEN

'The Finest Air in the Universe'

By the 1880s the policy of Fleetwood, wisely, was to offer a quiet, family holiday rather than attempt to compete with Blackpool. The Promenade was widened and extended. Theatres and concert parties provided entertainment. The Whitworth Institute progressed from Meeting Hall to Library and after a long struggle the Victoria Pier was built. Sea and flyer trips to Blackpool, Wardleys, Barrow, Ulverston and the Isle of Man carried hundreds of holidaymakers in boats whose names became household words; *Viking, Lady of Mann, Lady Margaret, Lady Evelyn.* The Belfast boats, the famous 'Dukes' operated for eighty-five years, their removal in 1928 to Heysham being one of the hardest blows Fleetwood ever received, for they provided much employment and were a success.

The ferry service prospered until the 1950s. Originally using rowing boats, the Croft family from Over Wyre operated the service. It was advertised in 1906 as 'Ferry from Fleetwood every fifteen minutes.' The earliest steam ferry boats were *Playfair* and *Guarantee.* Empowered by an Improvement Act in 1894, the Local Board and later the Urban District Council ordered in turn *Onward, Lune, Wyresdale, Progress* and *Bourne May.*

The Fleetwood ferry boat Wyresdale.

The Wyresdale, *1928. This ferry boat made crossings to Knott End. On one occasion a boiler explosion on board this vessel killed a man.*

Fleetwood's favourite Isle of Man Steam Packet Company ship, Viking *in dry dock. The town was presented with the ship's bell when* Viking *went out of service.*

Fleetwood beach and early promenade. Decimus Burton's summerhouse tops the Mount.

In 1942 Fleetwood's surveyor Mr W. Melville wonders if this area was terminal moraine or the site of a Roman port, Portus Setantiorum? Sailors talked of 'a great wall which rises above the water like the Loch Ness monster and has man-made rings'. Here, the paddle-steamer Zion Hill was wrecked and forests once grew.

The ferry boats were met by wagonettes and charabancs. Crossing to Knott End had become as traditional as visiting the Docks. Pilling, Preesall, Nicky Nook and Windy Harbour were all picnic spots within easy reach.

Amenities such as piped water, improved town gas, electricity, electric telegraph, hospital, libraries, tramway, improved fire-fighting services, sewerage and roads all came in time, many having to be fought for and the account of how these were achieved would make a book in itself. To pay for these services, rates were increased. The building programme took four stages. Following the early start cut short by lack of funds, the first accretionary period was 1878–94 when 907 houses were built, the new docks supplying impetus. These were mainly terraces, spaced grid-plan pattern, Decimus Burton's original radial style being too expensive and wasteful of space. 1894–1920 was again followed by a depressed period coinciding with troubles in the fishing industry, but latter years have seen the building of large housing estates swallowing up the farms. Shakespeare Road Estate, designed by Patrick Abercrombie in 1925, developed under the Town Planning Scheme to cover the acres of Warren Farm. Chatsworth and Larkholme (the old Larkham) estates have spread on the west side.

The formation of the Fleetwood Estate Co. led to the leasings of large areas though there was little following of the original layout. Regular block units of houses appeared, but the fact that some control existed did prevent the disjointed urban sprawl characteristic of some towns. The Fleetwood Estate Ltd, the new company formed in 1901, offered areas in Rossall Beach and Cleveleys, echoing Sir Peter's desire for town dwellers to buy seaside residences. A grand plan to erect a Hydro in the Larkholme area never got beyond the drawing board. Church Street and Dock Street ceased to be the hub of the town. By 1885 Lord Street (renamed East and West Streets in 1910) had become the main shopping centre together with Poulton Road, once the country road and main entry into Fleetwood. In 1892 the new Co-operative Emporium opened (demolished in 1973). Shop fronts were fitted to houses and by 1929 Lord Street had four banks compared with only one left in Dock Street. The shift was partly due to the loss of the railway station in front of the Crown Hotel and the coming of the tram road in 1898, a further stimulus to trade. It swept down Lord Street to the new station, completely missing Dock Street which, with the once-bustling, brightly-lit Church Street, faded like a ghost.

Processions to celebrate Hospital Saturdays, Sunday School occasions or important changes in the town's history, like the Granting of the Charter in 1933, were happy affairs with well-groomed horses, ribbon-decked, their brasses shining like gold, milk floats with their churns burnished, elaborate tableaux. The whole town joined in with brass bands from all over Lancashire.

The Local Board of Commissioners, cut down to twelve members, continued to govern the town until 1888 when the Local Government Act constituted County Councils. On the passing of the 1894 Act the Board was superseded by the Fleetwood Urban District Council consisting of eighteen members. Three wards were created but when Fleetwood was incorporated as a municipal borough by Royal Charter the Council consisted of six aldermen and eighteen councillors with six wards. Some twenty Acts and by-laws since 1842 were involved in this progress.

The first child to be born in Fleetwood was Isabella Roskell on 9 October 1837, daughter of Robert, a customs officer who lived in Church Street. An examination of population figures shows how the town grew:

1851	3,121
1871	4,428
1891	10,031
1901	12,093
1920	19,038
1933	23,430
1976	28,600

Rateable Value rose from £11,344 in the mid-nineteenth century to £99,822 in 1920. In 1974 under local government reorganisation Fleetwood became part of the Borough of Wyre which has a population of 98,800.

Growth rate was obviously affected by the economic situation. A few years after formation the resort declined, port activity became the mainstay and the new docks in 1877 brought a wave of prosperity. The end of the nineteenth century saw another decline, but as cargo trade fell away the fishing industry came into the ascendancy to make Fleetwood the third most important fishing port in the country and the premier hake port. In this lies the foundation of Fleetwood's true prosperity, an unexpected source with small beginnings. Fishermen in the early days had no thought for railways and markets. They used

Trawlermen and their catch, 1915.

Jacinta *FD 159 sails through the dock entrance for the last time on a commercial fishing trip.*

The Mayor of Wyre, Charles Stebbing, and the late Sir Walter Clegg attend an auction when trouble was brewing with Iceland, February 1968.

A fish auction, 1910.

The last fish auction at Wyre Dock.

City of Selby *FD 8, on the slipway, December 1917.*

small-masted sailing boats, venturing 15 miles into Morecambe Bay, catching a few stones of fish and selling locally.

Danger went hand in hand with the job. To the simple fisherfolk the sea with its inevitable association of separation, reunion, death and eternal life, was a significant calling; the mysterious voices of the waves all part of a great design. Mourning had a merciful clause of acceptance overlayered with superstitions which have still not disappeared. The folklore of the sea has a particular fascination, one story being that stormy nights set the church bells of the submerged Fylde villages ringing.

Because of receding tides at Southport fishermen from Banks, Marshside and North Meols settled in Fleetwood in the early 1850s. Fishing smacks were built on the beach by firms like Singletons (founded 1842), Armours, J. Gibson &

Steam trawler Star of Freedom FD 200 *at sea.*

The three-masted Valkyrien *at Fleetwood Docks.*

Sons, and to satisfy demand also at Freckleton and Glasson Dock. A steady ninety smacks was maintained until the introduction of steam trawlers reduced the numbers. Eventually *Harriet* and *Margaret* alone were left from the galaxy of names – *Ada*, *Alicia*, *Ariel*, *Amethyst*, *Badger*, *Beaver*, *Christine*, *Comet*, *Confidence*, *Corsair*, *Cygnet*, *Devonshire Lass*, *Druid*, *Desdemona*, *Excelsior*, *Gem*, *Gratitude*, *Ida*, *Livonia*, *Louie Rigby*, *Moss Rose*, *Zephyr*, etc. – some went for houseboats, some were left behind the dock, a sad mass of twisted ribs. Some day their story must be told and that of the long-lived breed of courageous, God-fearing people – the inshore fishing community, mainly Primitive Methodists, who lived in the Upper Dock Street area (now Mount Road). The spirit of this resilient group sharing a common interest epitomised something of what Sir Peter had dreamed. Racing to the fishing grounds, the fleet made a wonderful sight, but it could return with sails torn to ribbons and a town stilled with fear if foul weather blew up. In December 1894 a photograph of all the widows and children of 'Black Friday's Gale' was issued in the *Fleetwood Chronicle*. That Christmas was a time of deep sorrow and such grim reminders that the price of hunting fish can be the lives of men are woven into the tapestry of the town.

The brave exploits of the trawler *Gava* at Dunkirk and the *Clotilde* who rammed a German U-Boat in 1918 off Scotland and captured her commander are worthy of mention – quite a change from the 440 halibut brought home by *Kitty* and *Defender* in 1909 or the astounding catches of hake in 1905.

Concern about the over-fishing of the seas was felt in Fleetwood as far back as 1920. Prolonged dispute with Iceland and the mounting fear of let-down by the Common Market on this issue came hard on a population that had served a long apprenticeship and know fishing to be the toughest job in the world.

The foundation of the modern industry was laid in 1891. Firms connected with the industry grew – The Great Grimsby Coal Salt and Tanning Co., Isaac Spencer, James Robertson, Taylor & Tomlinson, Devon, Lancashire, Tattenhall, Sun, Iago, Active, Clifton Steam Fishing Companies, J.N. Ward, Trawler Supply, J. Marr & Son and many more. Gourock Rope Co. replaced the old rope walks which disappeared, for hand-making could not compete with machines nor could cottage industries such as net-braiding, replaced by big firms like Boris.

The churches of different sects were among the earliest buildings to appear in Fleetwood for Sir Peter 'offered a site for the erection of a church to any religious body possessing a sufficient number of adherents to justify the action.' When ways of liquidating the debts of town buildings were being sought by Charles Hesketh he was told '. . . it would give double the amount but Sir Hesketh's arrangement was to give the plot for the chapel. His plan in all cases was to give the ground for places of worship and from that he will not alter . . . for he conceives that where a large population is gathered together it is much better that all classes should be accommodated to their own religious views.' Frederick Kemp wrote thus in August 1850 and throughout the years, founded on this spirit, good feeling has reigned among Fleetwood's chapels and churches which have continued to expand with the growing population. In the same spirit the schools were fostered. One of Sir Peter's expressed aims was 'to devote sincere attention to the school and the poor.' Richard Fleetwood, an antecedent who died in 1695, had founded the first Charity School at Preesall and there is an endearing story told of Sir Peter calling on Mrs Cumpsty, wife of John who marked out the streets of Fleetwood by plough. The Cumpstys were ardent Methodists and in one room in their house on the corner of Dock Street and Church Street Mrs Cumpsty opened the first day school. Sir Peter called to find the small room crowded with children and he offered her the use of the small building opposite St Peter's Church on condition that she would clean and put it in order for services on

Sundays (this was 1839 before the parish church was built). From such friendly beginnings grew the schools of the town.

And the people themselves? Neighbourliness is still remarked upon although the boundaries of the town have spread considerably and no longer can it be said that 'everybody knows everybody else.' Nicknames, traditional among the fishing fraternity, die hard, especially among the backbone families – the Wrights, Leadbetters, Rimmers, Bonds – colourful and humorous examples of these are Couch Wright, Smasher Jackson, Red Neck Lombard, Slippy Wright, Rhubarb George, Russian George, Rising Tides, Whiskers Hesketh, Bung Colley, Cloggy Bond, Mudd Leadbetter, Pepper Wright, Crunchy Rimmer and Rough Jack.

The North Euston Hotel was sold to the government to open in 1861 for military purposes. 'Fleetwood awoke one morning to find itself famous as the seat of the School of Musketry' wrote Charles Hesketh to his wife, with a dry

Queen Victoria's visit to Fleetwood, a drawing by John Eastham, 1847. This shows the crowds who waited for two days. On the left is Queen's Terrace.

reference to his brother as 'the sanguine enthusiast.' Martial music filled the
town. The fishermen had inglorious fights with the soldiers; lifeboat occasions
and even children's parties were enlivened by Sousa marches. Lieutenant–Colonel
Vasey Ash, observing that the bracing air acted on his men like a tonic, declared
Fleetwood 'one of the finest places for health in England.' Seekers after this air
have included actors, writers, politicians and artists. Mrs Molesworth and Judge
Parry came regularly for long stays. Samuel Laycock, Lancashire dialect poet, was
for two years curator of the Whitworth Institute. Well-known visitors and natives
have included Sir Matthew White Ridley, Lord Stanley, the Duke of Windsor,
Lord Derby, the Duke of Kent, Princess Margaret, Lord Benares, Lord Hill,
Stanley Baldwin, Dr Edith Summerskill, Sir Fred Parkes, Sir John Parkinson,
Noel Le Mare, Percy Mather, Belle Chrystall, Edward Heath, Gracie Fields and
George Formby. When Queen Victoria came in 1847 it was the first time she had

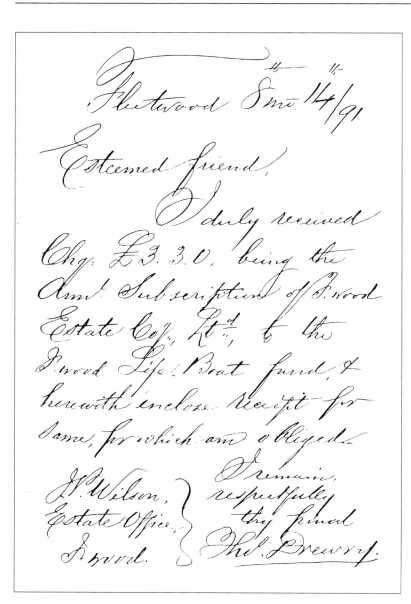

A. Thomas Drewry was a Fleetwood Commissioner. His shop on Dock Street supplied the coffee for Queen Victoria on the royal yacht. He also collected subscriptions for the lifeboat.

visited the Duchy of Lancaster. She sent out for freshly-ground coffee to Drewry's shop in Dock Street and Prince Albert got up at 6 o'clock to view the layout of the new town from the Mount.

The pioneers of Fleetwood's trade and industry were an array of colourful characters. William Porter came in 1841 and two years later started the *Fleetwood Chronicle*, the first copies of which were sold by William Whiteside, town crier.

Victoria and Albert, the Queen's yacht, which brought the royal family to Fleetwood via Scotland and the Isle of Man.

Printer Porter's son John wrote 'The History of the Fylde of Lancashire'. Joseph Walmsley and Joseph Preston came in 1836 and 1847 to found firms still in existence. Commissioners Esau Carter Monk and John Noblett who was killed by one of the early box tram cars were well-known figures, as was John N. Clarkson, Headmaster of the Testimonial Schools, and Martha Mason, the town's first librarian.

One would expect a fine record of seamanship from a town where it is said that the men have salt water in their veins. Well-known Master Mariners were Messrs Hesketh, Grimshaw, Dennison, Mason, Whiteside, Poole, Dixon, Mann, Fish, Cowell, Bond, and Iddon. Captain Iddon was ninety-one when he died and had commanded various schooners engaged in coastal trade.

Three generations of Singletons were involved in navigation by sail. The first unloaded cargoes at Skippool before Fleetwood was built. His son David sailed on the *Utility* as ship's boy, aged only ten, and his son Thomas Miller Singleton visited Malta, Spain, Philadelphia, Bermuda and Halifax, Nova Scotia, in masted barques. Captain William Miller ('Dusty') was one of a number who ran away to

Pandoro roll-on roll-off ferry.

sea and travelled the world. One Master of the *QE2* was Captain R.H. Arnott of Rossall Grange Lane, Fleetwood.

Thomas Lambert, to mention but one descendant of the pioneer townsmen, lived until he was ninety-five and had a host of memories – of John Dunderdale the lamplighter, the building of Victoria Pier and Jubilee Quay, the Italian with the dancing bear who used to cross over to Knott End in the ferry boat, the coming of the circus to town and the Grand Procession, the Old Gaff Theatre, Solly's Pierrots, the Convict Ship, carols in Albert Square accompanied by the town's brass band, well-lit ships on their nightly crossings to Belfast, sailors home from foreign lands with gifts of turkish delight, Florida Water, cinnamon, ginger from China. Different cargoes thundered the motorways to supply the Pandoro roll-on-roll-off terminal at Fleetwood Dock administered by British Transport Docks Board, where the *Buffalo* and *Bison* left daily for Ireland with the punctuality of railway trains. Helicopters assist lifeboat rescues and serve an offshore rig. Throughout the season brightly-dressed holiday crowds spill like a river across Dock Street into the famous market. All of which is not such a far cry from the lithograph and prospectus advertising Peter Hesketh's purpose-built town of more than 160 years ago.

ELEVEN

The Black Diamonds Mystery & Others

So much for past history. Now what of present, for the present has to be considered, bearing in mind that none-too-easy sliding into a brave new world which followed the First World War and the Depression. Cataclysmic events had hit the whole country bringing changes undreamed of. Still shouldering legacies from the past, Fleetwood town was hard hit. A spate of mysteries made headlines, some not without humour.

Boys braving the Spartan life of Rossall School thought nothing of 'A jollie swim in the Irish Sea, then beefsteaks for breakfast', new boys faced an initiation period, Lady Fleetwood, a ghost spun from garbled history, haunted from the Gazebo on a hill outside Rossall Hall to float down the secret passage to Burn Hall (a most unlikely story). She was, of course, buried in falling sand. Stories of legendary housemaster, Mr Sleape, must also have 'put the wind up' as if there were not enough gales already on the school's doorstep. They had braved a Scarlet Fever epidemic in 1844.

The school, however, prospered and acquired a swimming pool. No more plunging into the stormy sea! Nowadays, children aged three to eighteen years are accepted at Rossall School and many come from abroad. Copies of *The Rossallian* record how scholars fought for their country in two world wars. How many climbed the Rossall Beacon for a dare?

THE LANDMARK – ROSSALL BEACON

Was it unique? This question is often asked, for no one seems to recall having seen such a structure elsewhere, not even in illustrations. Long before Fleetwood boasted two fine, stone lighthouses – indeed long before Fleetwood existed, a large cone-shaped wooden pyramid, like a primitive 'Jungle Jim' climbing frame, was sited in a field on Rossall Grange Farm, close to the sea, about a mile from Rossall Hall. The date of origin of the landmark is uncertain but it was probably 1740 when the Lancaster Commissioners put it there to guide ships heading for Lancaster Port and Glasson Dock.

More than one of these beacons, in spite of their immensely strong timbers, was washed away because Rossall Point was so wild and stormy, and the sea continually encroached. Before the great boulders, those natural sea defences had been carted off to make into the streets of Liverpool, Barrow natives could hear the distant roar and see across to Morecambe Bay's southern limit where a white line of foam broke over Rossall Point. They could even forecast the weather by its

Originally there were two gazebos flanking the mound in front of Rossall Hall. This drawing by Ron Baxter shows the remaining one.

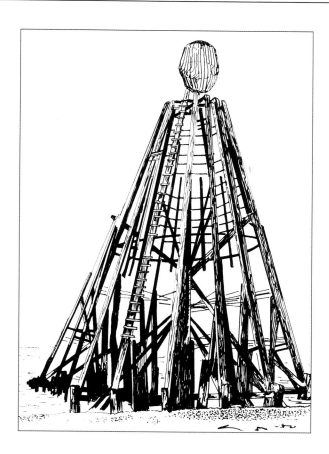

The Landmark, Rossall Beacon drawn by 'Sea Dog' (John Charles Houghton). The first one was erected in 1740.

behaviour. The Landmark, Rossall Beacon, was the first guide the mariners saw, nearing home, after a voyage from the West Indies with a cargo of mahogany.

THE BLACK DIAMONDS MYSTERY

The 1920s evoke much nostalgia for they were hard times in general, unemployment being rife, but nowhere was it more so than in Fleetwood, where breakfast could consist of half an onion. Many children had no shoes; even in cold weather they set off to school barefoot. To get warm you ran hard or burned wood, peat or coal in a barred grate. Peat was said to warm you five times, when you cut it, when you 'winnow, robin and stack it', and finally when you burn it, but Over Wyre country was where the peat came from and many Fleetwood families had no fuel at all other than driftwood from the beach. Food, clothes and rent took the meagre income. You made your own entertainment in sing-songs round the piano, charades, Sunday School socials, long walks and processions, and if any mad spender went to a lantern slide show it cost all of twopence (children half price).

Eighty years ago a rusty Fleetwood dredger was clanking up channel on a grey tide. Wyre Dock had just received one of its periodic scourings to rid the base of old fishing gear, basses, pound boards, boxes and other rubbish that accumulated in its murky depths. That day's haul had brought up 50 tons of coal, lost over many months while 'coaling' was in progress. This process, necessary at every voyage for the coal-burning trawlers of those days, was speeded up by using double chutes. Inevitably some lumps fell overboard between the lines of trawlers waiting their turn prior to setting off for Iceland, Bear Island, the Faroes or wherever they were bound.

As they moved in the direction of Lune Deeps the dredger skipper's conscience was working overtime. Why should these black diamonds be lost for ever, dumped in the ocean, when friends and neighbours could not afford to buy coal although it was only 1s 9d a bag? He passed the pier, a long one in those days before it was burned down, and about 200 yards further on he ordered the load of coal to be dumped on the mussel beds. News spread fast, or had someone already known? From all parts of the town people came with handcarts, wheelbarrows, bassinettes, soapboxes on wheels, buckets, spades, shovels, forks and rakes; bare hands clawed the precious coal into hessian sacks and bags. Even darkness did not stop them. Lanterns, oil and carbide lamps were brought out to lighten the scene as the work went feverishly on. Whole families were conscripted for the task and load after load was taken back to their homes. Most enterprising were those who went out by boat as the waters fluctuated, waiting for the tide to refloat and return them to the shore. One very old lady wearing a shawl was seen to make several trips using an old sack which she carried back over her shoulder crammed with as much as she could stagger with. In local parlance Fleetwood became 'Klondyke' until the memory faded, but the name of the man responsible was never breathed. Certainly his employers took no action and maybe he was even commended behind the scenes by them and by grateful residents with warm hearts and for once – warm bodies.

THE *LADY ANNE* MYSTERY

Lady Anne; a good name for a graceful yacht. I must have been four when I first heard my parents talking about the mystery of the *Lady Anne*. I pictured a tall, pale figure ghosting in the gloom of some dark corridor, but why were they linking her name with that of the *Marie Celeste*?

Every year we visited Blackpool and Fleetwood during the illuminations time and every year it varied, but the trip to the peninsula was pure magic because we saw 'real' ships coming and going, among them craft like *Lady Anne*, *Fidelis*, *Juanita*, *Mabel*, *Minaroo*, *Moonstone*, *White Rose* and *Jean*, but none ever sounded as special as she. The name and the mystery surrounding her enthralled me then as it does now. Little did I know that fate would put me in charge of the local history for that area and that I would never miss an opportunity for research or conversation on the subject: conversation with seasoned mariners, some now seventy and eighty years old, but wonder still lingering in their tones and sooner or later one will growl from the depths of his beard: 'Another *Marie Celeste*'. Here then is the saga, the tragic conundrum of *Lady Anne*, not one bit abated with the passage of years, for the mystery has never been solved.

On 7 October 1931, *Lady Anne* set sail from Barrow to return to her home port of Fleetwood. A 30ft-prawner designed for use in the shallow, stormy, tricky waters of Morecambe Bay and built originally by Crosfields of Arnside in 1904 for Mr William Hornby, she had been taken over first for racing by Charles Tatham, an expert yachtsman, well known in the area. Carvel-planked and cutter-rigged, she always gave a good account of herself.

In the 1928 Annual Race to the Isle of Man for example, *Lady Anne* swooped in like a bird – second. Again and again she proved herself capable of coping in first-class style with the capricious Irish Sea.

Her next owner, Mr Paul Drummond, was connected with a long-established Fleetwood family, the pioneers of which had actually worked on the first buildings of the town. On that last fateful voyage in 1931 Paul was joined by his cousin Alan, a solicitor, and the four-man crew included two other family connections, Mr Higham, aged twenty-three and Timothy Swarbrick, seventeen, from Wardleys, where *Lady Anne* was usually moored.

The three men were all experienced yachtsmen, Mr Higham being on leave from the Merchant Navy. Around 9 a.m. that morning *Lady Anne* had headed for the open sea and Barrow, apparently having a good trip, for her arrival was recorded. Fed and refreshed, the party of four completed their business. Four hours later *Lady Anne* sailed up the River Wyre as though knowing her way. Turning at Wyre Light, fouling no buoys, she sped down channel to ground eventually alongside Fleetwood Pier. She was seen to glide flawlessly downriver, completing the trip, but on investigation not one of her crew was found to be aboard. Nor were any of them seen again. What had happened?

Lady Anne was partially disabled, though her sails were set. The yachtsmen had been seen to commence the homeward journey in their 7-ton cutter at about 2.30 p.m. from Barrow. Piel lifeboatmen, out for practice, saw *Lady Anne* making for Lune Deeps. All seemed well. The next to see her were the keepers of Lune Light. Noticing she was unmanned, they flew distress signals to warn those on shore. The steam trawler *Agnes Wickfield*, coasting down channel, saw *Lady Anne*'s masthead broken, the canvas sails displaced. Drawing alongside her, the trawlermen's shouts were met with silence.

News spread fast and hundreds of people visited the spot near the pier, guarded by police. Men worked till midnight dismantling *Lady Anne* by the light of lamps. The mast with its trailing gear and sails was first unstepped and the boat fittings removed. Calmly, stoically, fathers Higham and Swarbrick stood by with other relatives, hoping with every passing moment that somewhere, somehow, survivors had been picked up, but the first light of morning broke with no news.

Theories advanced by well respected local seafarers, men with lifetimes of experience between them, concerning a danger patch near Lune Deeps, declared that a typical, deadly characteristic was presented by Fisher's Brow Patches, a shallow stretch where the water suddenly varied from 23 fathoms to just 7. At exceptionally low tides such as that October's sudden bad weather could spawn danger. In such a heavy swell as was running that Wednesday afternoon the yacht could have bumped at this point, flinging out all occupants. That it was an eerie spectacle to see the yacht with not a soul on board, pursuing its homeward course down channel, all agreed. Some people even advanced a sea monster story, that all four had been swallowed up and lost without trace, yet, on a more practical level, at no time could the wind be said to be dangerous to men experienced in handling yachts. The short squall that had sprung up was well within their capabilities and *Lady Anne*'s seaworthiness.

C.E. Tatham, the previous owner, said 'Something terrible must have happened, and not far from the mouth of the Wyre. Two years ago I sailed her in the Fleetwood to Ramsay race and she was the only boat to finish. There were heavy seas on that occasion.'

Mr G. Skeogh, a workman on the sea defences, reported sighting *Lady Anne* at 4 p.m. making for the Light, struggling but keeping her course, turning well with the current as though being properly handled, then beaching herself between the pier and the piles. 'When I saw her she seemed to be answering to someone at the helm and she did that all the way. I saw nothing of men being thrown out near Wyre Light. It was uncanny. Had she been steered she could not have kept on a better course.'

Further examination showed that there were no scratches on her to prove that she had struck the bottom. What little damage there was had been done as she lay off Fleetwood Pier. Barrow seamen, equally experienced, believed that *Lady Anne* was over-canvassed when she set out, sailing with a slack mainshaft. Months later the men who did the repairs at Barrow reported that the main sheet was bent backwards as though tremendous strain had been put upon it. They believed that *Lady Anne*, sailing at speed, had fouled some object with such resultant force that all four crew were flung into the water and drowned.

But why were their bodies never recovered? And how did *Lady Anne* manage to sail on for home with such aplomb and accomplishment? It is an unexplained secret of the sea which never loses its intriguing lure.

HERE COMES THE SEA

The first intimation of real danger came close on midnight when the hurricane with the tide at its height (42ft) reached 90mph. Eerie blue flashing lights, the 'wow, wow' of a police car's loud hailer fluctuating in volume as the gale-tossed words set my heart beating. What was it? Anxious to know, I opened the window. The hurricane pounced and I was powerless. In seconds the glass would have shattered had I relaxed my hold. My numbed gaze fell on a man racing before the tide. Thank God it was my husband – and never had I been so glad to see him! Perfect timing was his strong point!

'Imminent danger of flooding in this area – stay indoors go upstairs,' bawled the police and then they dashed off into the night. Speeding up the drive my husband saw that I had no chance of closing that window. From outside he banged the window shut.

I dashed to let him in. 'The cello, the safe, papers,' he gasped. Grabbing a basket, we crammed in important documents and shot upstairs with the musical instruments, collecting family photographs on the way. There was a smashing of glass as the porch caved in, ripping the front door off its hinges. The garage door swivelled to let in a rush of seawater that battered down the rear door, gullied through the back porch, lifted a storm door off its hinges and careered on to flatten a 6ft garden wall. Two bicycles, buckets, coal, tools and paint tins swirled from the shed.

Suddenly all the lights went out but I groped for a torch and took what food I could reach from the top shelves in the kitchen. Weirdly the telephone rang. It was the last call we were going to get for two months. Our son coming from university was meeting water, water everywhere. 'Don't come home, the sea's coming in, go to friends,' I shrieked, and the line went dead.

Smoke began to pour through the floorboards. The carpet heaved like quaking sands beneath our feet. In between bouts of rushing like maniacs to seize what portable articles we could, we stared in speechless horror. Gently, my husband said, 'We can't do anything – come upstairs . . .'

From a bedroom window we looked into the pitch blackness. Waters were rising, foul, muddy, evil smelling. Our house was literally in the Irish Sea and, as our eyes became accustomed, it was plain that sea defences had been torn away. Cars were submerged, sprawled in all directions or bumping like mad things in garages, as were freezers. Not a soul could be seen and throughout that awful night during which the gale battered the house fit to blow in the windows and suck off the roof, hour after hour sounding like demons, no one came near. What, we thought, had happened to the old people in the bungalows?

Mercifully the fabric of our house held. By early light, still unable to believe the catastrophe which had taken place, we viewed the hideous mess left by the sea's retreat. Smelly, thick, sludgy mud covered carpets and furniture.

'Walking the plank' and spotting a lifebuoy in our garden we joined neighbours for a good moan. Their gas cooker still worked and we had a loaf of bread and a bottle of whisky found bobbing on the flood! As the morning advanced, concerned friends arrived to roll up their sleeves and help. An electrician got our cooker part working and six sturdy men and true dragged out the lounge carpet. The pile grew as the day advanced. So did the crowd of unfeeling sightseers. Successive days brought looters to our bonfire-high pile of carpets, fridge, freezer, furniture, vacuum cleaner, electrical appliances, bric-a-brac.

As everything downstairs was contaminated, I decided we must eat upstairs and use our daughter's wedding presents stored at home while she and her husband were abroad. So it was that with bare floorboards and not a downstairs door that would close we drank from crystal glass and ate from best china. We had one chair lent to us. I recalled Edward Lear's poetic lines:

> Two old chairs and half a candle
> And a jug without a handle.

I got a roaring fire going with our coal scattered over the back garden. We baked potatoes and boiled pans gypsy-style. Returning weary one day after sorting insurance, we found a delicious parcel of roast ham tied from a doorknob! It was a time when you found out who your friends were. It took three months to get the house refitted, refurnished and redecorated after which we had to start on the garden!

I shall never forget the terror of that fearful night and the recent tsunami disaster brought it all back. Amid a plethora of jobs, one ridiculous memory sticks – cleaning thirty-two pairs of shoes! Sadness lay in the loss of precious books, school prizes and sentimental treasures, films and slides. Impregnable sea defences, costing millions of pounds, have now been built but eventually many moved away, unable to blot out the memories and the fear of a repeat performance!

Between the sea and our family lies a love–hate relationship but to some families, uninsured, it was worse. We heard of nervous breakdowns and people sitting amid the chaos just drinking to forget. Yes, you could say it was an emotional experience, and it was another prophecy fulfilled that its timing came fifty years after what was always called Fleetwood's Great Flood.

MARGARET V. *RELIANCE*: THE 1903 BOXING DAY RACE

In the early years of the twentieth century the white-winged fleet of fishing boats at Fleetwood was dwindling rapidly. This from a port which in the nineteenth century could boast a fleet of ninety fishing smacks, many a boat being famous in its own right; *Harriet, Onward, Milo, White Rose, Ida, Bluebell, Ambrosine, Wonder, Polly, King David, Red Rose, Moss Rose, Surprise*. Their well-loved names were legion. What a sight it was when they set out on a favourable tide from Jubilee Quay, some with freshly barked sails which gleamed red in sunsets.

Wives and children standing on the traditional spot by the Lower Lighthouse waved goodbye but never with white handkerchiefs (too reminiscent of shrouds). The sea which gave a living could be cruel. Black Friday was still in mind and the December blizzard in 1894 when six wives lost their husbands, three mothers their sons and nineteen children were left fatherless.

James Armour and W. Singleton of Adelaide Street with John Gibson & Sons and Robert Newton of Dock Street were the main ship and boat builders but there were three others, not to mention ship chandlers, sail makers, rope and twine makers, etc.

Annually on Boxing Day the cream of these lovely craft would gather for the racing event of the year and 1903 produced the most exciting race of all.

Regattas, started by Mr Stoba, were a feature in Fleetwood's heyday but the Boxing Day race was the event of the year. Used to early rising, most of the populace would be tramping up the Mount by 7 a.m. or assembling on the promenade.

There were fears that the wind was not strong enough that morning but by 8.40 a.m. contestants were lined up in readiness, although some had to be towed to the starting line. Fortunately the breeze freshened. The Mount buzzed with speculation, bets being laid on the possible winner. Amid experienced fishing families Abram, Roskell, Wright, Leadbetter, Bird, Hesketh, Bond, feeling ran high. Pride was at stake but two names were on every lip, the *Margaret* and the *Reliance*.

Reliance FD 210, a two-masted ketch-rigged fishing smack built by Gibson & Sons had been launched by Mrs Liver on 23 October 1903 and wonder of wonders – she was fitted with the famous Stoba-designed keel. Mr William Stoba, who worked for Armours boat builders, was well known beyond Fleetwood and his name is still one to conjure with among today's yachtsmen. A Stoba-designed keel meant speed.

The first leg of the 36-mile race involved the passing of Fairway Buoy and Shell Wharf Buoy off Rossall. Down the coast they beat onwards to Nelson Buoy, Lytham. This was the turning point and excitement mounted as the two notable craft began to battle it out. In the lead by eleven minutes was the 71ft *Reliance* but *Margaret*, the older, well-tried craft skippered by J. Colley, famed for hake landings, cut the lead by four minutes on the homeward run.

Like seagulls, *Margaret* and *Reliance* skimmed up the coast. They tacked and tacked again in search of favourable winds. In the long discussions that followed many a seadog thought that if only *Margaret* had been able to use a jib-sail she

Margaret *at Glasson Dock, 1900.*

Reliance *FD 210. (Ted Ramsey)*

would have won. As it was, *Reliance*, skippered by Mr R. Wright, lengthened the lead again, eventually passing Knot Spit fifteen minutes ahead of *Margaret*, completing the race in three hours three minutes.

For forty years, *Reliance* remained a hard working fishing vessel. Most, like the *Harriet* FD11 who outlived them all and is still with us today as a museum piece, succumbed to a diesel engine and a winch to haul in the catch, thus ending the romance of sail.

The fate of *Reliance* seemed inevitable – to end her days a rotting hulk behind the Elevator, but she was bought by Frank and Ann Davison for £1,450. They dreamed of sailing round the world and spent two years fitting *Reliance* out. Secretly they set sail one night leaving her port of provenance for ever. A mighty squall off Portland Bill smashed to matchwood the once-proud winning yacht. Mr Davison was drowned and Mrs Davison, an amazingly lucky survivor, told the story in her book *The Last Voyage*.

All of which brings to mind the mariners' heartfelt prayer 'Lord be merciful – my ship is so small'.

'I AM FLYING LIKE A BIRD ACROSS THE SEA'

In 1842 a service was commenced from Fleetwood to Mona's Isle, now commonly known as the Isle of Man. The fare was 4s, 6s first class. Indeed, the Mona's Isle Company existed as early as 1829. During those years a strong tradition of service and friendship steadily built up between Fleetwood and the island. Thousands of passengers were carried across in fair weather and foul.

Individual boats were famous, of which TSS *Manxman* was to become the only remaining passenger steam ferry in Britain. Her sister ship, *Mona's Isle*, was scrapped in 1980 and there was speculation in the shipping world that *Manxman* would follow her to the breaker's yard. Although capable of carrying 2,303 passengers, on her last sailing from Fleetwood there were only 490 on board, the revenue from which was not sufficient to pay for the bunker oil to fire her turbines. Saved by a group of businessmen and enthusiasts, she was eventually berthed at Preston Dock and billed as 'Europe's last remaining steam-powered passenger liner'. She became a day visitor centre and museum and was also used in film sets, notably *The Missionary*, *Chariots of Fire* and *SOS Titanic*. It is with much affection that I recall going aboard *Manxman* to meet Judith Roberts of Radio Lancashire when my book *Shipwrecks of the North West* came out. Built by Cammell Laird of Birkenhead at a cost of £847,000, she was launched on 8 February 1955. Of 2,495 gross tonnage, with a speed of 20 knots, in her heyday *Manxman* had a crew of 68.

The noteworthy steamer whose excellence had contributed to many enjoyable holidays in the Isle of Man calls to mind another conspicuous vessel among a great line. The *Viking*, built in 1905, was the first turbine steamer owned by the Manx Company. On 25 May 1907 *Viking* made her fastest crossing from Fleetwood, Lune Buoy, to Douglas Head in 2 hours 22 minutes, achieving an average speed of 23.2 knots. Season after season thousands witnessed her departures and arrivals, so that when at last she was withdrawn in August 1954, appropriately her bell was presented to the town of Fleetwood. An inscribed mounting made from her timbers was placed below the bell and gave details of her distinguished career, including war service, but was wrongly inscribed 'average speed 33.2 knots'. For some time the magnificent bell in silent indignation pronounced this a real clanger, but happily the newly designed Viking Bar in the Marine Hall, one of the many attractions of the 1982 Maritime Heritage Year, put the record straight.

Another final slipping of moorings and sinking of hearts came about on 12 September 1965. It was 'Goodbye Ben' when *Ben My Chree* sailed at midnight from Douglas to Liverpool with the last of the Grand Prix visitors. After forty years' service to the island, the oldest and best loved of the Manx steamers was sold. She was the first crack ship to have one funnel and many new navigational aids such as searchlights, fog signals and a depth sounder that could be used even when the ship was going at full speed. My father, without hesitation, always cited *Ben My Chree* as his favourite ship, a view shared by Merseyside ship spotters interviewed at the time on BBC *Look North*. She did 200 trips a season and carried millions of passengers from the Irish Sea ports to the Isle of Man. The *Ben*'s first passage, made on 29 June 1927, was historical in that coincided with the day after a total eclipse of the sun, which her many passengers had travelled north to witness.

Memories linger of beautiful wood panelling, the gold and white ceiling of the first-class lounge, glorious rose and lavender decor and her slim, white hull. On her last trip she was captained by Commodore W. Cain, reputed during his twenty-two years in charge to have carried more passengers than any ship master in the company. The last weekend of *Ben*'s career was marked by a gathering of the World Ship Society.

A later *Ben My Chree* played an historic part on 1 July 1979, the year of the Manx Millennium. The Viking longship *Odin's Raven*, specially designed and built for the occasion, was sailing from Norway to the Isle of Man. On passage from Ardrossan to Douglas, in an unscheduled stop off Port Patrick, Captain Jack E. Ronan brought the *Ben My Chree* alongside the longship to enable passengers to take photographs. He was presented with a photograph of *Odin's Raven*, signed by all the members of her crew, a uniquely historic occasion.

Slipped moorings of another kind occurred on a wild and stormy night in January 1976 when the *King Orry* broke away in Glasson Dock and wandered onto the Cockerham Marshes, but that is another story altogether in the history of the great Manx ships.

The crew of the Duke of York *on the Fleetwood to Belfast service, launched on 23 February 1894. In the white apron is the stewardess, Mrs McCaffrey.*

Talking of storms, the equally famous Belfast boats whose long, proud Fleetwood service closed on 28 April 1928 also faced calm and tempest in their thousands of crossings of the Irish Sea. In late December 1894 Captain John Cook, a tough and courageous Scottish sea veteran on the Fleetwood to Belfast run, had the unenviable task of battling against a cyclone. At 120mph it struck the north-west coast of Lancashire, breaking among other things the Meteorological Society's wind-recording instrument on the Mount at Fleetwood. Anxious crowds gathered near the railway station, straining their eyes towards the horizon, fervently hoping for the safe arrival of the *Duke of York* with its 400 passengers all longing to get home for Christmas.

Leaving Belfast at 8 o'clock in the morning, aware of the imminent gale, Captain Cook soon considered making for the Bahama lightship. In worsening weather the starboard engine stopped, but fortunately the engineer managed to get it going, so with plenty of coal available, they tried for Fleetwood. The ship battled on towards Walney, by which time the coal was beginning to run low. Discounting the Morecambe Bay Lightship because of its uncertainty, Captain Cook resolved to make one last attempt and with all in readiness for emergency he ran for the only landmark, Wyre Light, just managing to clear the bank and gain the comparative safety of the Channel. At long last, at precisely 4 o'clock in the afternoon, amid cheers they made landfall with ninety terrified female passengers, several injured crew and everything movable having been washed overboard. It was the worst cyclone that either chief mate Captain Higham or Captain Cook had ever experienced. In fact they learned afterwards that the shock of it had killed Christopher Smith, Captain of the Morecambe Bay Lightship.

Forty letters of gratitude were sent to Captain Cook from passengers thankful for their safe deliverance. The directors of the Lancashire & Yorkshire Railway Company and North Western Railway Company granted an extra week's wages to the crew. The historic cyclone in the Irish Sea was a popular topic of conversation over Christmas dinner that year!

Captain John Cook was not forgotten. At one time master of *Thomas Dugdale*, a position he held for 34 years, he crossed the Irish Sea 8,000 times, becoming Commodore in 1875. Upon retiring, he lived in Fleetwood and saw the final Irish sailing in 1928. Two years later he died at the age of 83.

The words of the seventies hit song seem to be particularly appropriate to Fleetwood:

> 'I am sailing . . . stormy water
> I am flying like a bird across the sea'.

The fisherman's good luck omen on board Dean Swift, *1927. The bird, a gannet, was adopted for the voyage.*

JOHN GIBSON: MASTER SHIPBUILDER

A member of one of the best known and highly respected families of nineteenth-century Fleetwood, John Gibson became one of the town's most famous shipbuilders. Born in Kirkcaldy in 1815, the year of the Battle of Waterloo, he came to Fleetwood at the age of 22 to work on the pile-driving which was essential in the construction of the Preston and Wyre Railway. John lodged at the nearest available place, Twenty Houses, Burn Naze, which a hundred years later became the site of ICI. From here, he tramped to work every morning across the sandy peninsula within the sound of the sea.

John was soon to make his mark. In 1846 the *Fleetwood Chronicle* reported that he chaired a meeting held at the Fleetwood Arms to discuss a testimonial to Henry Smith, a pioneer who worked so hard to keep the Preston and Wyre Railway going throughout the difficult years and established Fleetwood as a packet station for the carriage of the Royal Mail to Belfast.

John's first shipyard was near the old fish warehouse, from where vessels were dragged across the quay and launched by being dropped broadside into the river. From here he moved to opposite Queen's Terrace where he built a patent slipway. By 1857 he had formed a partnership with James Butcher which was to last for three years. Fishing smacks *Surprise*, *Cygnet*, *Ellen* and *Ann* were the first to be built for Meols fishermen who, on Sir Peter Hesketh Fleetwood's invitation, had settled in Fleetwood when tides at Southport began to recede. When the partnership was dissolved, James Butcher retained the block-making interest, which John later took over on Mr Butcher's death.

By 1861 the shipyard of John Gibson & Sons was sited where the P&O ferries now dock. The Fleetwood improvement commissioners received complaints from residents of Queen's Terrace about, 'an unsightly timber shed and sawpit', but John sharply pointed out that shipwrights were necessary to a port. Fleetwood was beginning to boom, so why complain?

What an exciting time it must have been when ships of all shapes and sizes were being built on the Wyre. Barquentines and brigantines were arriving on every tide. The year 1862 saw the launch of the 107-ton schooner *Richard Warbrick*, whose figurehead was carved by a Workington man in the likeness of Mr Warbrick's son. Shingle on the slipway delayed the launch of the magnificent oak vessel, but this was achieved on the next high tide by Agnes Warbrick, with a bottle of champagne.

The following year, the windows of Queen's Terrace were crammed with people watching John's second smooth launching, that of the schooner *Sarah Ann Dickenson*. Mrs Whiteside of the Fleetwood Arms laid on a sumptuous dinner at which John spoke in praise of the schooner's rigger, Mr Coulborn: 'he had brought out the beauty and sailing capacity of the vessel and has had so much to

Queen's Terrace, designed by Decimus Burton.

do with the final cut as the tailor has to do with the making of the man'. It was the launching of the schooner *Agnes* that attracted the greatest ever number of spectators to Fleetwood.

By 1867 John Gibson was fighting the Gas Company on behalf of Fleetwood residents. Not only did the gas smell awful; it was too highly priced. Furthermore, how dare the company close Cop Lane, a public right of way! He fought also to protect the Mount, which was constantly threatened by encroaching seas. It was he who urged the commissioners and Sir Peter Hesketh Fleetwood to do something.

By 1868 the 158-ton schooner *Ellen Widdup* was on the stocks, following in a blaze of glory, schooners *Useful*, *Elizabeth and Ann*, *Agnes*, and the two-masted ketches *William and John* and *Ezra*. On 26 February 1869 *Sarah Ann Widdup*, another schooner for Warbricks, was launched. But it was 1870 that in retrospect proved a sad year. The fine three-masted schooner *Manchester* with the steam tug *Jabez Bunting* in attendance had been launched without a hitch. At the Crown Hotel dinner the toast was 'to the lovely child of hoary old man Manchester and fair nymph Fleetwood'. Just fifteen months later the ill-fated *Manchester*, on a voyage from Stockholm to Barrow-in-Furness with a cargo of steel, disappeared without a trace. All the crew were lost.

The pinnacle of John's career was marked by the barquentine *Emily Warbrick*, the sixteenth vessel from Gibson's yard. Launched in March 1872 after eighteen months in construction, she was the largest ever built in the town, 140ft in length and 23ft 4in in beam. The population turned out in force. The band of the 47th Regiment of Euston barracks filled the salty air with stirring music and at

Emily Warbrick, *Fleetwood. This famous topsail schooner was built on the beach at Fleetwood.*

1 o'clock in the afternoon, as the tide reached 20ft, the daggers were knocked from under her keel and she glided down the slipway to the tune of 'Rule Britannia'. This time the shareholders and friends proceeded to the Royal Hotel where the beautifully scrolled menu showed forty items from which to choose. The pride of the whole town was expressed in the *Emily Warbrick*, 'a vessel as beautiful as the young lady whose name she bears'. That young lady was eventually to marry the schooner's commander, Captain Poole.

John went on to buy the Bonded Warehouses in Dock Street but industrial action set trade back when a number of his workmen left to earn higher wages at the shipyard in Strand Road, Preston. Although trade recovered, with the launch of the schooner *Esther* in 1875, John, who died in 1877, never saw the opening of the long-awaited dock at Fleetwood, but his sons played a big part in the festivities. The chandlery shop opposite the stone quay where schooners were fitted out after launching was similarly resplendent.

The last of the large schooners built on Gibson's riverside site, the *John Gibson*, christened by Miss M.A. Porter, daughter of Edmund Porter, glided down the slipway in 1878. In June 1890 Gibsons suffered a great blow. Their extensive premises, situated only 40yds from two gas holders, caught fire. Inhabitants of the nearby houses fled in terror to the shelter of the Mount. Fortunately the wind fanned the flames away from the gas works. The town fire brigade, dock fire brigade and military fire brigade battled nobly, but had to abandon all hope of saving Gibsons' mainly wooden premises in order to safeguard surrounding property. It was 8 o'clock the following morning before the fire was finally put out.

The firm never really recovered and the family never forgave the Railway Company who had shown no sympathy for shipbuilding and twice displaced the firm. However, under James Gibson, the business, famous for its high standard of workmanship, carried on. The yard concentrated on small craft: half-deck boats, pleasure steamers, prawners, fishing smacks and ferry boats. Wealthy yachtsmen from Barrow to Bangor and beyond aspired to owning a Gibson-built racing yacht, especially when the renowned designer William Stoba was involved.

In 1902 Gibson's shipbuilding business changed hands, purchased by Liver and Wilding.

George Gibson, son of James, born in 1851, lived until the age of 85. A Freemason, he started his career in Drewry's shop, the grocers which supplied Queen Victoria's yacht with freshly ground coffee on her visit to Fleetwood. George, who quickly rose to own his own business, was an exponent of Tonic Solfa singing. Four of the family sang in the choir at the congregational church.

This was indeed a family that made a great contribution to the town. Without them the exciting days of sail would not have been half so exhilarating!

TOPSAIL SCHOONERS IN PORT

Strolling along the pleasant promenade at Fleetwood, gazing across Morecambe Bay to the Lake District and Furness Fells it is hard to imagine that one and a half centuries ago the new town of Fleetwood welcomed ships from all over the world.

The 1840 harbour improvements made by Captain Henry Denham were a great success, involving three lighthouses, and iron wharf mooring buoys, beacons, dredging operations and warehouses for bonded goods. Belfast traders, said the *Railway Times*, preferred the port on the River Wyre to Preston because it was at once open to the sea.

The first shipyard was Mr Halliburton's, from where *Atlas*, ordered by the Preston and Wyre Railway Company, was launched on 25 April 1838. Shipbuilding was carried out on the shore, J. Gibson & Sons having a yard in 1863 opposite the Canshe Hole. 1843–4 was a bad time generally for shipbuilding. For something to do, 300 ships anchored off Ichaboe Island off Namibia to collect tons of penguin guano, some of which was brought to

A Fleetwood topsail schooner. (Ron Baxter)

Fleetwood. Sugar, flax, timber, grain, spirits and cotton came from the West Indies, America and the Baltic, the first cargo of the *Diogenes* was celebrated by the occasion of a public dinner at the Fleetwood Arms in 1846. Bumpers of wine were passed from hand to hand; hopes for the future high. Considerable coasting trade was built up and by 1870 schooners sailed or appeared on every tide, *Lancashire Lass* being one of the fastest. Many of these belonged to Fleetwood. Two early ships to be built were *Manchester*, who disappeared on her first voyage, and *Ellen Widdup*. Some of the master mariners lived in Walmsley Street, among them Hesketh, Grimshaw, Dennison, Mason, Gornall, Cowell, Sumner, Nuttall, Anyon, Fish, Ball, Roskell, Whiteside and Winstanley. A host of topsail schooners crowded the port: *Resolution*, *Village Girl*, *Blue Jacket*, *Eclipse*, *Esther*, *Emily Warbrick*, *Richard Warbrick*, *Red Rose*, *Elizabeth Ellen*, *Richard Fisher*, *Bessie Jones*, *Nanny Wignall*, *Polly Whitaker* and *Saxon Maid*. The crews, between four and six in number, took great pride in their turnout. Decks were well scrubbed, brasswork shone and a carved, painted figurehead usually decorated the prow.

The 167-ton *Emily Warbrick* was a famous Fleetwood vessel built by Gibson & Sons in 1872 and one of a small fleet which included *Richard Warbrick* and *Agnes Warbrick*. These, like *Englishman*, under Captain Green and later Captain Whiteside, travelled from Fowey to Fleetwood carrying china clay. Pig iron was brought from the Clyde. *Emily Warbrick* did the South Atlantic run for years, her first ship's master being W. Poole. When he saw the carved figurehead depicting Emily Warbrick, he wanted both the ship and the lovely girl, and was lucky enough to win them both. At 105ft 6in long and 23ft 3in wide, she was later renamed *Lost Horizon* and fitted with diesel engines. Homeward bound from the West Indies in May 1938, she was burned out, her crew being rescued by a Swedish steamer. The Wyre Shipping Co. Ltd of Edmund Porter and Richard Warbrick & Co. in 1880 were registered as owners of thirty-seven schooners ranging in size from 86 tons (*Nanny Wignall*) to 200 tons (*Lizzie Porter*). *Red Rose*, *English Girl* and *Dairy Maid* were among them.

Another famous shipbuilding firm was that of James Armour. The family had a long, interesting connection with the town. James Armour, along with his wife Ann, came to Fleetwood from Londonderry in 1847. He was a blacksmith by trade. Born in 1817, he died on 24 January 1875. His son James married Elizabeth Gill and they had eleven children, one of whom, another James, married Catherine Whiteside. They had fourteen children. This James recorded in his diary 'started work for my father on 28th December 1886, aged 13 years. John Armour, my father's brother died on 3rd January 1869, aged 39. He was one of seventeen survivors of SS *London* which foundered in the Bay of Biscay 1866, but he died at sea while on a voyage from Panama to Melbourne and was buried at sea'. There is also a reference to William Stoba, a perfectionist among ships' architects, who designed a number of well-known craft for Armours and commenced work there on 5 September 1905. Two famous cutters built by Armours and designed with Stoba's curved forefoot, which made for better handling and speed, were the *Alpha* and the *Kindly Light*. The *Kindly Light* first belonged to the Bristol pilot Louis Alexander, but was sold in 1955 to Mr C. St John Ellis of Eton College. He sailed 50,000 miles in her before loaning her as the founder vessel of the Ocean Youth Club in 1961. She has since introduced 20,000 youngsters to the sea. Renamed *Theodora*, she was first home in the Tall Ships' Race to Corunna, awarded the Romola Cup and the Royal Cruising Club's Challenge Cup for crossing the Atlantic in twenty days both ways. Hammond Innes, President Nixon and many other famous personalities have been on board and signed her visitors' book.

James Armour's ledger is starred with the names of ships built or repaired in Fleetwood: *Comet*, *Brilliant Star*, *Bispham Jessie*, *Oyster Girl*, *Petrel*, *Pioneer*, *Syrene* and *Zoe* among them. Details of the repairs take one back in history: 'to *Nimble*, 1881, £32 17s 10d for oakum, pitch, spikes, nails, leather, elm, oak, greenheart, birch, pine, wedges, dead eyes, mast hoops, copper tacks, bolts, spars, blocks, Jigger Topsail, Jigger Reef bull's eyes, fenders.' One new 9ft spar cost 3d and a child's coffin 10s 6d.

To see these topsail schooners safe into port was *Falcon*, the pilot boat F1. Her figurehead was carved by L. Fitzsimmons at a cost of £3. 'Her decks were kept well clean and varnished twice a year, bulwarks, winch bits, companionways and skylights all bright and burnished. Nothing I can say about her is too good, for I always thought so much about her', said her pilot, Lancashire man Mr Gerrard. His ancestor, John Gerrard, had piloted Queen Victoria's yacht on her visit to Fleetwood in 1847.

What adventure stories were played out on long, hazardous journeys during the days of sail defies the imagination. Details of the stories alone are interesting. In 1864 *Cicero* set off for San Francisco with 2 sides of bacon, 2 barrels of pork, 4cwt of bread, 50lb of Cooly Rice, 8 bottles of pickles, 55lb of Crew's tea, 60lb of coffee, 2 cases of lime juice, half a box of candles, 4 bottles of whisky, 4 firkins of butter, 2 casks of molasses and 10 cheeses.

Much attention had to be paid to sails during a voyage. Bolts of canvas for repairing and making sails were loaded and these conjure up foresail, topsail, main royal, moonsail, crossjack, topgallant and other fascinating titles.

Captain Monk of the *Cicero* had to go round Cape Horn: 'I hope to hear that you have not caught over-much round the Horn', wrote a fellow sea captain. 'Keep your temper old fellow and when Frisco is reached, before signing Bills of Landing, read carefully'.

Added to this was the important skill of stacking cargo, correctness being a vital necessity (especially when rounding the Horn). However carefully this was done, things could still go wrong in rough seas. A good sea captain knew when to pile on canvas and when to stow it away. The lives of men and the safety of his cargo depended upon him. He had to be a superman. Little did the Fleetwood boys who ran away to sea realise what they were letting themselves in for!

SET IN STONE

In the early hours of a cold winter's morning two distinguished Fleetwood firms set about the formidable task of moving a carved 4-ton stone. This was no ordinary stone. It had been kindly given by the British Transport Docks Board to the Fleetwood Civic Society and there was a mystery about its origin. What was no mystery was the fact that this giant object was intrinsic to the town of Fleetwood, sure to be of interest to local and railway historians alike and thus was worthy to be moved from its ignominious site behind the docks, a site where once

Part of Fleetwood station before demolition in the 1950s.

stood Fleetwood's very first railway station which was little more than a wooden hut when the first train chugged over the timber trestle on 15 July 1840. That exciting opening day for the Preston and Wyre Railway deserved better. For years Sir Peter Hesketh Fleetwood had striven in sickness and in health. He had given money until he was nearly bankrupt in order to build the line.

The stone, however, could not have been delivered for that day. Could it have been intended for the 1850s station opposite the Crown Hotel, which was erected on Dock Street when the railway line was re-routed around Kirkscar Bay? Tons of stone had been washed from the embankment in the making of this route. In the short space of six years the timber trestle had become unsafe and a terror to lady passengers when the tide was rolling in. However, from the symbols chiselled into the stone it seems more likely that it was intended to find a place in the scheme of things for the grand yellow-brick station erected at the other end of Dock Street, by which time Fleetwood had become a busy port, an important railhead and a holiday town. The symbols set in stone represent a train leaving a tunnel, a steam packet paddle-steamer and the Legs of Man. Fleetwood had a connection with the Isle of Man dating back to 1842.

In October 1877 Wyre Dock was opened. The Preston and Wyre had become the Lancashire and Yorkshire Railway Co. Significant also was the fact that similar stones were built into the Grain Elevator (pulled down in 1940) although these were smaller and differently designed. No mystery about the date of the Canadian-style elevator! The year, spelled out in white tiles, could be deciphered miles away.

Carved by the Stocks Brothers, it is probably one of the earliest railway commemorative stones still in existence. Why was it delivered to the old site on

Lancashire and Yorkshire Railway commemorative stone, 1870. This now resides in Euston Park.

the docks, did it come by sea or by rail, and why did it lie there, 'unwept, unhonoured and unsung'? So many brave ideas floundered in the early days through lack of money, but indications are that the stone dates from the 1870s when Fleetwood was booming. Why was it not given a place of honour?

Through the valiant efforts of Brown and Jackson Ltd, of Copse Road, and Messrs James Robertson & Sons Ltd, of Wyre Dock, the stone was conveyed to Euston Park and, in a memorable ceremony on 1 May 1976, it was handed over to the townspeople of Fleetwood in the presence of the late Walter Clegg MP, the late county councillor William Brown, Deputy Lieutenant of Lancashire, His Worship the Mayor of Wyre Borough Council, Councillor R.C. Snape and British Transport Docks Board Manager Mr A. Winfield.

And there it is to this day for all to see, a poignant piece of Fleetwood's history which at long last found a more honoured resting place and gave us all something to think about.

THE WARRENHURST DIARY

Few things are more tempting or more morally forbidden than peeping into a private diary. Although filled with the littleness of life, that cosy state which humans treasure only when it appears to be threatened, private diaries may also yield high adventure, intrigue or delicious indiscretion, all motivating ingredients to the curious delver. None of the latter, however, are seen in the diary of Fanny Jameson, great grandmother of Frank H. Tolley of Wythenshawe, but the steady troop of day succeeding day, orderliness, the round of the seasons, neighbourliness and a sense of accomplishment in work well done still make satisfying reading and give a very good idea of life in Fleetwood during the year 1874.

The diary, which turned up among family papers, was beautifully transcribed by Mr Tolley and extracts deemed worthy of preservation in the Queen's Archives at Windsor Castle. As starters for the year 1874, whetting the searcher's appetite, we find that in January, soon after Christmas Day Fanny 'wrote to the Queen and Madam de Strauss'. What about and did they ever meet?

Captain John May Jameson, born about 1833, hailed from Ireland, becoming Civil Engineer to Sir Peter Hesketh Fleetwood, and he obviously chose a good wife. He and Fanny resided at Warrenhurst, a large, isolated house situated in the area now called Poulton Road. Old Fleetwood inhabitants can remember an ornamental lake and peacocks strutting on the lawns when Captain Baugh, Commandant of the Belfast Boats, lived there. Long before on this spot had stood East Warren Farm, whose tenants were instructed by Trinity House to whitewash the walls as a landmark for mariners, it being the first building visible when approaching by sea. One of Fanny's ancestors, lawyer Mr Elletson who worked

An 1860s trip to Furness Abbey ruins. Fanny Jameson (second lady from the left) was from Warrenhurst, the wife of J.M. Jameson, civil engineer to Sir Peter Hesketh Fleetwood.

for the Heskeths, valued East Warren Farm on 24 June 1824 at £360 10s, at the same time putting a price on the rest of the Warren upon which was to rise the town of Fleetwood – £59.

The Warrenhurst Estate in the days of Fanny's diary consisted of a 'Commodious Dwelling House, two vineries, Conservatory, Stables, Coach House, Shippon, Outbuildings standing in twenty-six acres of Meadows, Pasture and Garden Land', this detail being revealed in the plans and particulars of Wednesday 25 March 1885, when part of the estate was sold, and by which date Fanny was dead. In April 1890 an attempt was made to sell the remainder. Warrenhurst has since been pulled down and the land became Fleetwood's Memorial Park. Flags from the old kitchen, where pies and pounds of gooseberry jam were made, pieces of stonework, bricks and other fragments were built into local gardens and are all that now remain of it, but Fanny's diary vividly evokes the daily round and her husband's involvement in constructing Fleetwood, especially the Rossall sea defences, the completion of the Promenade and the never-ending need for embankments to protect farms such as Larkham. Where the latter stood is now covered with sprawling Larkholme housing estate.

Captain Jameson, staunch Conservative, pillar of society and a very busy man who in the course of his duties travelled to Manchester, Preston, Liverpool and London, made a declaration on 5 July 1875 under an Act from King William IV's reign: 'I am now, and have been for the past fourteen years, agent to the late Sir Peter Hesketh Fleetwood, Baronet, also to the present Sir Peter Louis Hesketh Fleetwood and to the Trustees of the Fleetwood Estates.' Two years previous to Fanny's diary he actually planned an iron way between both sides of the River Wyre 'at the same time providing for the passage up-river of shipping'. He enlivened board meetings by taking along his dog and he made arrangements for regiments of volunteer soldiers, 600-strong, to encamp near the town. The diary makes reference to many more of his activities, but Fanny herself was never idle.

Although no doubt considered 'gentry', she was a thrifty housewife who wasted neither materials nor time – 'busy repairing old nightgowns', 'made a dress with Mrs Jim', 'busy darning', 'in spite of a headache darned the eiderdown', 'put up white curtains'. When the bees swarmed it was Fanny who dealt with them. She supervised the stacking of the wood pile and even picked caterpillars off the gooseberry bushes.

Entries reveal the unfolding of the year, the exploits of her son John Gardner Hope Jameson, affectionately called 'Garnie', a mischievous nine-year-old who, in a trip to Parrox Hall where Fanny was born, fell into a pond on 21 December, his birthday, but by the 30th, all forgotten, he was 'skating on a pond with the Lloyds.' Chopping wood, Garnie received a badly-cut hand but was soon out and about again with his mother, paying social calls on the doctors' and clergymen's wives or receiving such visitors at Warrenhurst as dashing Captain Jarvis and his lady, Mr and Mrs Jim, 'Mifs Carter and three little Carrs', Mr Carr – himself an important Lancashire and Yorkshire Railway official, Mrs Antrabus or Captain Nightingale and Mr Seagrave of the 95th. One day the Lord of the Manor, Sir Peter Hesketh Fleetwood called with 'little Louis'. If the weather turned wildly inclement visitors 'staid alnight', such was hospitality in the good old days. Cryptic initials and sobriquets made the reader wish to shout across the years to Fanny. Who was NIK who dined with the Masons on Thursday 3 December and who was Mr Jim? What repercussions arose after the Valentines were sent to Clara and Percy on 14 February? Did it spark off a marriage or a Thomas Hardy situation as in *Far From the Madding Crowd*?

When Mr Brown came ferreting rabbits inevitably Fanny prepared six rabbit skins. Fur tippets were fashionable, or would they make gloves for Garnie? On Thursday 17 December when Major and Mrs Fitzroy spent the day with them at Warrenhurst, a pure white peacock was delivered.

Stirring martial music on church parades, all the colour and pageantry of a barracks town, visits to Preston, Garstang and Furness Abbey, Easter holiday in

Ambleside, exercising the dogs on West Shore, attending balls at the North Euston Hotel or concerts at the Whitworth Institute, going on board the *Thomas Drysdale* docked at Fleetwood, or seeing her husband off on the train ('JM went to Preston at 10.50 appealing against taxes'). Never bored or complaining, the theme of the diary is energetic application to work all year long. In June, as in December, 'Clara and I were very busy making 33 yards of muslin frilling', 'Covered dining room chairs with leather', 'busy with skins', 'took a tin of honey and put the bees back in their hive', 'JM and I walked to the Battery with Mrs Jim.' (A wooden battery of two 32-pound guns at the foot of the Mount belonging to the coastguards was used to train Naval Voluntary Reserve.) Satan never found mischief for Fanny's hands for they were never idle. A modern theologian would find interest in the detailed noting of texts, preached each Sunday. The Jamesons were regular churchgoers. From Fanny's day-to-day comments the life of the town is brought into sharp focus. Remarkable for its absence of criticism or self-pity, the diary reveals her as a neat, practical, no-nonsense, kindly lady, the salt of the earth.

Fanny was an Over-Wyre lass who enjoyed Beethoven, indulged neither in private daydreams nor drama but got on with it and was all the happier because she had no time to 'moon', but she had time to copy up JM's accounts!

One can only speculate as to whether Captain John May Jameson who married Helen at St Luke's Church, Southport on 25 November 1887 was as fortunate in his second marriage. The industrious and cheerful Fanny of the diary, who died in 1876 aged only thirty-nine, little dreamed that a hundred years later her year's round would still be of interest even beyond the confines of her small cosy world.

To the Gallant Crew of the *Gava*

A much delayed letter from Frenchman Alfred Dequinnemar of 232 Rue Coli, Wasquehal, arrived in Fleetwood on 7 November 1944:

> Please accept the homage of all my comrades of the 15 Company Tank Corps who thanks to the heroic crew of the *Gava* were able to leave the hell of Dunkirk and were safely landed at Ramsgate on the evening of 1 June 1940. We shall never forget that day and less still, the courage and endurance shown by the crew during the tragic day of evacuation.

> Hurrah for *Gava* – My gallant friends and your little ship, what became of you?

A good question for a time when British history was being made. Known as Operation Dynamo (26 May–4 June 1940) news of it hit the astonished crew of the *Gava*, unloading their catch of fish at Fleetwood. They discovered that the Royal Navy had commandeered their fishing vessel and it was to sail from North

End in command of six trawlers on 27 May under sealed orders, arriving at Dover on the 30th and finally Ramsgate where she found she was to proceed to Dunkirk to assist in the evacuation of the Allied Armies.

Gava, along with five other trawlers *Droon*, *Edwina*, *Evelyn Rose*, *Jacinta* and *Velia* was skippered by Fred Day, Lieut. F.J. Jordan RNR was Senior Officer.

The crew of the *Gava* owned by the Clifton Steam Trawling Co. was as follows: Fred Day (Skipper), A. Blanchard (mate), Ernest Norton (bosun), Albert Heselhurst (chief engineer), T. McConnell (second engineer), Amos Sumner (gunner), Reg Gowan (gunner's mate), Arthur Durme (wireless operator), Harry Gawne (deckhand), John Jones (deckhand) and G. Eastwood (cook). There was also a fireman known as 'Piano Jock'.

The crew's first sight of devastated Dunkirk was one of sunken ships, the shore seething with embarking troops making for larger ships. Smaller boats sailed between them.

Through the surf, troops waded out to these smaller boats, oily waters up to their chests, their guns held high over their heads. Parts of German aircraft littered the beach and the droning Luftwaffe swept the skies above beaches and a smoking town. Dead bodies floated on the waves and the noise was deafening as bombs clumped down and guns from the ships responded.

Suddenly a message came that no ships were to proceed further unless capable of 20 knots. There was consternation on the bridge of *Gava* but the naval lieutenant signalled back that *Gava* could do 20 knots proceeding at full steam engine flat out at 10 knots!

Chief Engineer Heselhurst must have been saying his prayers! Amos Sumner takes up the story,

There was no-one in the outer harbour as *Gava* entered. Dirty water was littered with wreckage lapping gently against the dead gun crews of a Destroyer sunk to her gun platforms. We tied up at the stone pier. It seemed lonely, a sunken vessel lay athwart the lock gate of the inner harbour but we hadn't long to wait.

The remains of the 15 Company French Tank Corps appeared and embarked in orderly fashion. 376 Frenchmen scrambled aboard as the sky filled with German aircraft. The naval lieutenant ordered our gun crew to stand by 'Independent fire commence.' We had had only 3 weeks gunnery training at Liverpool prior to going to sea on armed *Gava*. Johnny Jones breech loader and Harry Gawne had also been on that Course. Together we taught the other members of the gun crew! Evacuation was completed in an hour, magnificently conducted by a French Officer who, as *Gava* set off, refused to come aboard but stood to attention and saluted *Gava*, the last ship to leave the harbour, which was still under fire.

Nearby, a French destroyer had been dive-bombed, her hull disappearing and the oily waters were crowded with desperate swimmers. We picked up over 100 of them.

They were dazed, shocked, covered in oil and burnt.

Arthur Dunne (wireless operator) Harry Gawne and John Jones jumped overboard to rescue three French sailors in danger of drowning.

The fishermen's contempt for the lieutenant turned to admiration. His excellent gun crew was complimented. They brought down 3 planes and possibly a fourth with their 12 pounder.

From the time *Gava* left England to setting a course for return to England; home and beauty, calm, Skipper Fred Day had been on the bridge continuously. Our small ship was covered with survivors, all available space taken. Only the gun platform was kept clear and Cook was continuously in his Galley, brewing up tea for thirsty crew and thankful Frenchmen.

That night at Ramsgate there was a party aboard ship. The cook poured ten bottles of wine taken from Dunkirk cellars into a bread mug and mixed in 2lbs of sugar and a dozen eggs. One and all needed a pick me up!

The Frenchmen wanted to stay in England. 'Long live England' being their cry, but, on recovery, they were sent back to France and sadly some were taken prisoner there. *Gava* had transported 365 men back to the UK.

As for *Gava*'s crew, they were hailed as folk heroes, three being decorated: Dunne, Gawne and Jones.

The Navy's official report on the other trawlers

Jacinta Fleetwood Trawler

1 June	0725	Left Ramsgate for Dunkirk in company with other Fleetwood trawlers, under the command of Lt. F.J. Jordan, RNR
	1125	Arrived Dunkirk
	1126	Embarked about 150 French Colonial troops
	1126	Proceeded
	1700	Ran on a submerged wreck, about 2 miles south of the N. Goodwin L.V., and took on a list to port of about 25 degrees
	1701	The tug *Java* came to her assistance, and decided to remove *Jacinta*'s troops before attempting to refloat her. This was accomplished with the assistance of Nelson's M/B which had left Ramsgate at 1645 en route for Dunkirk

| | 1800 | The M/L Fervent (Lt. Cdr WRT Clements, RNR) returning from the Dunkirk area found the *Jacinta* in the Downs, drifting with the tide and deserted, but apparently seaworthy. Lt-Cdr Clements allowed her to drift to a safe anchorage, and then anchored her |
| 2 June | | *Jacinta* was towed to Ramsgate by one of the Fleetwood trawlers. She was found to be making a little water. Total: 150 |

Evelyn Rose

1 June	0725	Sailed from Ramsgate with other Fleetwood trawlers (see *Gava*)
	1125	Arrived Dunkirk
		Embarked 130 French troops
		Proceeded
		En route, lost a propeller blade on a wreck
		Arrived Ramsgate. Disembarked 130 troops
		Total: 130

Dhoon   Fleetwood Trawler

1 June	0725	Sailed from Ramsgate with other Fleetwood trawlers
	1125	Arrived Dunkirk
	1126	Embarked 130 French colonial troops
		Proceeded
		Arrived Ramsgate. Disembarked 130 troops
		Total: 130

Velia   Fleetwood trawler, Skipper J. Clarkson

This vessel went over to Dunkirk on 1 June with the Fleetwood trawler flotilla under Lt. F.J. Jordan RNR in ft. *Gava* (q.v.) This officer reported to Captain M. Harwich that the *Velia* did not embark troops, but that she towed the damaged Belgian trawler No. 26 to Dover
Note: No troops transported

Edwina   Fleetwood trawler, Skipper P. Bedford (?)

This vessel went over to Dunkirk on 1 June with the Fleetwood trawler flotilla under Lt F.J. Jordan RNR in ft. *Gava*. (q.v.) This officer reported to Captain M. Harwich that the *Edwina* was machine gunned and that 2 of her crew were wounded; also that she landed 120 French Colonial troops at Ramsgate
Total 120

Jacinta

FD 159. Built 1972 at Clellands Yard, a small ship division of Swan Hunter Ltd, Wallsend, Newcastle upon Tyne

Of all fishing vessels, *Jacinta* emerges as a name to conjure with. There have indeed been three *Jacintas*. The first *Jacinta* FD 235 being a coal-fired trawler was launched in 1915, costing £10,000.

She it was who joined the flotilla led by the Fleetwood trawler *Gava* FD 380, and like *Gava* she performed gloriously at Dunkirk on 1 June 1940, embarking 150 French troops.

The second *Jacinta* FD 21, now diesel powered, appeared in 1955, costing £125,000. She was one of the first diesels in the port. She was sold to Aberdeen in 1967 and scrapped in 1971.

The third, *Jacinta* FD 159, a stern trawler, costing £340,000 (now restored and preserved for posterity) was also destined to cover herself with glory. Throughout

A visit by international Rotarians to the Jacinta, *2006.*

A view of the deck of the Jacinta *en route to Spithead via Portsmouth, 2005.*

her career she proved to be a record breaker. Between 1972 and 1982 she sailed out of Fleetwood, one of the top-earning trawlers in the port. In 1975 she set a Fleetwood record for a wet fish trawler in a nineteen-day trip to Iceland which resulted in a catch of 188 tons of fish. On board was a sixteen-man crew, skipper Bill Taylor, mate Bernard Brierly, chief engineer George Thompson, radio operator Eric Christie, bosun Mike Southwell, ten deckhands and one cook. In 1986 she was the top British trawler catching fish worth £1.3million 'and she was the top-earning trawler again in 1994, this time the value was £1.94 million but this was only for ten months due to a major engine failure in October of that year. During her fishing career she caught fish worth £17.6 million.

A group of enthusiasts were anxious to preserve a Fleetwood trawler as part of Fleetwood's heritage. On hearing that this group was looking for a trawler, Alan Marr, Chairman of J. Marr & Son Ltd, offered the *Jacinta* to them. After much anguish they were offered *Jacinta* for £1. This historic coin is preserved on board in a glass case on display in the fish-room. In January 1995 the *Jacinta* Charitable Trust was formed with the aim of restoring her to her former glory. A group of

Jacinta *under tow to Manchester for re-engining.*

dedicated volunteers set to work after the crippled trawler was towed from Hull to Fleetwood. She arrived back in her home port on 15 February to a tremendous welcome. She opened to the public in August 1995 as a floating museum by skipper Bill Taylor. After a few years the trustees decided that the last part of the restoration jigsaw was to find a replacement engine. Mr Lionel Marr told me 'searches found a suitable replacement engine in the last working tin mine in Cornwall (South Crofty) and this was bought by the trust and arrangements were made for it to be installed at Manchester Dry Docks'. Once this had been carried out, *Jacinta* took to the high seas again to sail triumphantly into Fleetwood on 1 June 2003.

Since then, *Jacinta* has attended Maritime Festivals in Whitehaven, Hull, Grimsby, Barrow and Bristol. In 2005 she represented the Fishing Industry at the Spithead Review, 'Trafalgar 200', a great honour followed by visiting the International Festival of the Sea at Portsmouth.

The only alteration made to *Jacinta* is that the fish-room which held 230 tons of fish has been converted into an exhibition/social room and museum. There are

Jacinta *leaving Bristol Harbour Festival in 2005. The Clifton Suspension Bridge is in the background.*

many models and photographs of the trawler and the fishing industry on display. Guided tours are conducted by local fishermen all of which adds to the attraction and gives a true story of life at sea for deep sea fishermen. The Fylde Folk Festival hold annual concerts and the Trust hold a well attended Carol Service every Christmas. A volunteer's baby was christened on board. The ship's bell was used as the font. From the many thousands who have boarded since the glory years, praises such as 'History brought back to life – a marvellous tribute to our fishermen', show that thanks are due to the volunteers who worked tirelessly to restore *Jacinta* (another labour of love) and to the Trustees: Lionel Marr (Chairman), Tony Lofthouse, David Pearce and Mark Hamer, Peter Horsley was an original trustee but has now resigned.

Saved from the scrapyard she sails again. Hurrah for *Jacinta*!

THE OLDEST FLEETWOODITE

In 1927 the *Fleetwood Chronicle* reported on Mrs Jones who was born in Upper Dock Street on 21 September 1841. The headline was 'The Oldest Fleetwoodite' and the occasion, her eighty-sixth birthday.

Her lineage was quite remarkable, one of her ancestors being a Fylde landowner in the days of Charles II but the lasting association with her name is connected with the wreck of the schooner *Bessie Jones* named after Mrs Jones' eldest daughter.

Mrs Jones proudly told the reporter that she had 'never been away from Fleetwood'. Her grandfather had played the bassoon and violin in Hambleton Church in the days when a moat surrounded the church and there was no organ.

Her mother had married Thomas Blackburn who came to Fleetwood when there was talk of a new town being built on 'Wild Rossall Warren' and it was on the Warren that they settled. Thomas built houses in Upper Dock Street and carried on a grocery business. When Rossall School started in 1844, he supplied butter and other provisions for the staff and schoolboys. Always interested in

A lifeboat heads for the scene of the wreck of the Bessie Jones.

shipping Mrs Jones recalled that her father was known as a 'ship's husband'. He cultivated wasteland between his cottage and London Street and made a garden between the Copse and Poulton Road (this possibly became Strawberry Gardens in later years). Before the Local Board was formed he was one of the first Fleetwood Commissioners.

Mr and Mrs Richard Jones invested in sailing boats and it was on the night of 20 February 1880 that the schooner *Bessie Jones* was driven ashore and wrecked in a fierce gale, leading to a remarkable rescue.

She was a Fleetwood vessel carrying 200 tons of old iron rails. Robert Bickerstaffe, coxswain of the lifeboat *Robert William*, realised that it was impossible to use oars against the huge waves breaking on shore. It was against the rules but he ordered two single-reefed sails to be hoisted and, once away, these were lowered, the crew took the oars and battled for two hours to reach the *Bessie Jones* whose crew were clinging to the rigging for their lives.

Made fast by grappling irons the lifeboat was in great danger, banging against the *Bessie Jones*. Captain Pater and his men were rescued by lifeline. Sadly one member of the crew had already been swept away. The dangerous return journey had to be braved and lifeboatman J.T. Fish, as the furious sea suddenly set the lifeboat on its beam-ends, was flung out. Miraculously the next wave swept him back into the *Robert William*. He certainly lived up to his name!

The only possible landing place was St Annes on Sea and the coxswain made for that beach where a wildly cheering crowd had gathered to greet the heroes.

The *Bessie Jones*, 230 tons burden, 114 tons registered A1 at Lloyds was six years old at that time. Samuel Laycock, the 'Lancashire Laureate' wrote a poem about his friend J.T. Fish and the crew must have indulged in some leg-pulling. These unassuming men were true icons.

An historic postcard was printed by the RNLI and proceeds went for upkeep of the lifeboat. Further upkeep depended on Mr Drewry's meticulous annual collecting of subscriptions. Carnival processions on Lifeboat Saturdays added more but to be aware of all that gallantry, daring and self-sacrifice, going forward on such slender means must nowadays bring humbling thoughts.

FROM PORT FLEETWOOD TO FREEPORT FLEETWOOD

Sir Decimus Burton (Decimus because he was the tenth son) was the last great architect of the British Classical School and the first to refer to Port Fleetwood when the area designated for the new town was a wilderness of sandhills. He was a guest at Rossall Hall, drawing up plans.

Years went by and, once cargo trade slackened, it was quickly seen that the site was ideal for Arctic fishing grounds. Additionally, Faroese, Hebridean and Irish waters filled nets to bursting with large, white fish while inshore waters in

The author, Catherine Rothwell, with a Norwegian visitor at the site of the Freeport.

Morecambe Bay supplied shrimps, prawns and a grand harvest of herrings. The whole populace was involved in the many aspects of the fish trade especially when Fleetwood reigned as premium hake port in the whole country. But this too was to decline leaving large acres of brownfield sites.

Fleetwood Freeport opened in July 1995 and has been expanded twice over the following nine years. Built upon a former brownfield site, close to Fleetwood town centre, it comprises over 50 units totalling over 110,757sq. ft. At the site are restaurants, cafés, a picnic area and soft play area for children, the chance to tour *Jacinta* and to sport with butterflies at the Butterfly Centre. Freeport Fleetwood is popular not only with the locals but also with visitors to Blackpool, Lytham, Bispham, Thornton and far beyond the Fylde coast. There is parking space for 700 cars and ten coaches.

Add to that 'the finest air in the universe' and, juxtaposed, an eye-catching marina run by the British Transport Docks Board. Unique appeal! Small wonder

Aerial views of the Freeport at Fleetwood.

that an estimated 2.5 million people are visiting the centre annually, all of which would have gladdened Sir Peter Hesketh Fleetwood's heart.

Even Sir Decimus Burton, though he might not have entirely approved of the new millennium's mock New England style of architecture, would have rubbed his hands over 53 units covering over 10,000 metres, soon to be joined by Marks & Spencer and more 'names to conjure with'.

From Port Fleetwood to Freeport Fleetwood was smart town planning.

TWELVE

Eros & Marina

'How in the long ago, we laughed and loitered so,' chuckled my friend as we strolled the length of Fleetwood's splendid Promenade on a bracing sparkling day.

Across the estuary snow-sprinkled Lakeland and Bleasdale fells sprawled silhouetted, slate blue against a clear sky.

'No wonder he decided to build a port and seaside resort here.' We were touching on the founder of Fleetwood. Jack, who years ago emigrated and did well working for the Canadian Pacific Railway, now retired and a widower 'back home' was full of his roots' reminiscences. 'Fleetwood wasn't all fish,' he declared, unleashing half a century of instant recall on my startled ears!

As the sun went down and a flight of oystercatchers with their haunting cry skimmed low above the edge of the tide, 'that was an education,' I murmured.

Among his rich kaleidoscope of memories was one pioneer, George Laurie, Improvement Commissioner and chemist who patented coloured lights for the rescue of seamen. His pharmacy was at Manchester House in Dock Street, premises later taken over by J.J. Raynor – 'hats, caps and an excellent assortment of stuff and silks'.

Adelaide Street featured the Health Clinic selling Barker's Liquid of Life ('£1,000 if not genuine'). All the shops had slogans to quicken trade. Freake's of Lord Street had a Dance Frock Display ('no two frocks alike'). The Norway Freshwater Lake Ice Co. was situated in Upper Dock Street and there appeared in 1909 Dodsworth's Ice Café – 'the perfect place for a knickerbocker glory'.

The year 1926 saw the first Fleetwood Dog Show and it is worth remembering that in the 1930s Fleetwood offered the cheapest electricity supply in the whole country!

Shops vied in their display to capture attention. Tickles in North Albert Street had a fascinating mixture of magic lanterns and glass slides.

Jack remembered Howarth's, photographers and 'suppliers of limelight', but outstanding was Michelbach's pork butchers with its brass-fronted window and marble slabs. The Christmas display there was unforgettable and, if you were a little girl, so was that at Smyth's Bazaar. Jack had gone on and on as one idea sparked another and the years collided.

Following the blighted promises of the 1840s, the heartbreak and failing health of that fifth son, born Peter Hesketh, who made the town possible, the setbacks were numerous. There were those ever-present friends and foes, sea and sand to counter. There was the falling-off of cargo trade because of rivals and an inadequate dock. There was the loss of the prestigious Royal Mail route via Fleetwood and Belfast. Those magnificent screw-propelled steamers 'the Dukes' had achieved the open sea passage daily in five and a half hours, but in 1928, after almost a hundred years, the service ended. In those glory days, express trains left Fleetwood station, one of the finest in the country, every weekday except Monday, to London and all parts of Lancashire and Yorkshire. Gone is the yellow-brick station and the railway wagons that used to run alongside the steamers for quick transit of merchandise. Worse and beyond all that was the loss of men when fishing smacks and trawlers were wrecked – terrible days like Black Friday during the 90mph gales in October and December 1893–5.

Recent years have seen the demise of a great fishing industry with its ancillary trades but that spirit of true grit, that 'something in the air' referred to by an early magistrate and by our first Medical Officer of Health, Robert Adair Ramsay, kept on flourishing. Dr Ramsay maintained that even when food was expensive and scarce, the pure air blowing across the peninsula kept disease at bay, building healthy bodies and stout hearts.

My fascination in the sweep of the years focuses on the Fleetwood people, many who built up prosperous businesses single-handed. One may well be amazed at how many there were nestling in the shadow of a thriving fishing industry. Fleetwood became the premier hake port in the country through the enterprise of local man Sam Colley, and enterprise shines out from the shops and business premises of 1900.

In Warrenhurst Road, Joseph Barnes, joiner and building contractor, ran the Fleetwood Sawing and Planing Mill. The Portable Building Co. Ltd could supply 'a convenient and artistic residence' (three reception rooms, four bedrooms, bathroom, kitchen, scullery and usual offices) for £450. William Hodgkinson had a Mineral Water Works in West Street 'manufacturers of every description of mineral waters and the finest quality brewed ginger beer'. One must remember that East Street and West Street later became Lord Street, but Dock Street and Church Street were elegant shopping centres a hundred years ago.

Messrs Pomfret and Livesey, cash drapers and house furnishers, could be found at nos 31–4 Church Street offering 'the largest and best selected stock of household drapery and furniture in the Fylde district'. Indeed 'the acanthus wreath divine' decorated Church Street premises, as in ancient Greece!

The cheese factory in Poulton Road had thirty prosperous years shipping from Wardleys to Ulverston and Milnthorpe. Starting as a family concern under Stanley Bamber, the Lancashire Cheese Makers Ltd passed to Unigate Creameries which closed down in 1966.

Another Fleetwood product was Blezard's toffee. Boiling and wrapping took place in the first two houses in Hesketh Place off London Street and what a lovely smell there was to go to school on! Another industry was pursued at Shuttleworth's Flour Mill in Mill Lane which ran between Albert Street and Church Street. Bread was baked from the flour and taken by cart to soldiers under canvas near Rossall Grange Farm.

At the turn of the twentieth century a button factory was situated in Apex Buildings, North Albert Street. Fleetwood girls preferred this to Crowe's Milliners and Haberdashers in Blackpool who paid only 2s 6d per week. A 'nice place' with regular hours and Saturdays off at Apex you could rise to 15s a week. Staff were brought from Birmingham, including a foreman and his family to train the girls. Metal buttons for service uniforms were the main product but buckles were made and Miss Gytha, an elderly Quakeress, was the expert in 'japanning' – stirring thousands of buttons in a jet black mixture, then baking them in a huge oven. The girls were noted for singing at their work.

Marquis's Rubber Factory, for ever in trouble for its smells and outbreaks of fire, eventually blew down in one of the great gales but the Albion Steam Saw Mill kept going and by 1906 at the Coal, Salt and Tanning Co. you could buy 'Wyre Light' flake tobacco or dark shag for threepence an ounce. This went well with 'fine, fermented hop bitters' at ninepence per gallon!

The Fleetwood Cotton Manufacturing Co. in Styan Street covered an area of 1,896sq. yds and was advised by a Blackburn cotton manufacturer, quite a guru according to Fleetwood Estate Co. papers. Working men went to Lewis Alban, Blakiston Street for the finest hand-made clogs in Lancashire. (Jack could remember when men's shoes cost 2s 6d a pair!) and to Manchester House, Dock Street, for 6s moleskin jackets.

Fleetwood Salt Works was busy and out of town there was Rossall Brickcroft and Flakefleet Brickworks. A statement of bricks made from 1 November 1893 to 31 October 1894 at Flakefleet totalled 2,055,628! There was even a granite company that brought over masons from Italy. The ferry to Knott End did a roaring trade and there were many visitors.

Fleetwood was a good place to eat, noted for shilling dinners ('beef, mutton, lamb or pork with vegetables, bread, pickles and pudding') from Whiteheads, Adelaide Street, and a good place also to parade fashions bought from Turner and Hance . . . 'Mrs Rothwell [my ancestor?] looked well in grenat cashmere with velvet zouave edged with crystal and a grenat and white hat', reported the *Fleetwood Chronicle*.

As the decade swept in there was plenty going on and plenty of signs of the old established Fleetwood we knew and loved.

Only once, when I had to arrange a Fisheries Exhibition, did I enter the portals of the Great Grimsby Coal Salt and Tanning Co. Ltd. What a title – here was atmosphere! Within that dimly-lit, womb-like interior was everything a deep-sea fisherman could desire. What was that tangy scent? Chanel, eat your heart out! It was Stockholm tar pervading oilskins, sea boots, Fearnought trousers, smocks, socks, thick woollen stockings, guernseys, woollen caps, sou'westers in brilliant yellow, and a formidable array of masculine underwear, all necessary. They went to Bear Island and Iceland in those days, facing Arctic conditions.

It was like no other premises I had ever seen. Hanging from the ceiling a panoply of menacing gear and on the floor, coils of sisal rope. On the counter, villainous looking shag and twist tobacco in snake-like black lengths ready to be weighed and cut. It was a time when men were men! Above in Eddie Rigby's sail loft young seamen were shown how to splice wire and sew canvas. More maritime atmosphere! Plastered on walls and beams were photographs of every sailing craft the Rigby's had fitted out. Eddie skippered the *Zulu Chief* passing on his craftsmanship and sailing skills. Meanwhile, 'Old Bob' (could that have been Robert Wright?) sitting comfortably on a huge coil of wire destined for trawl warps held forth on 'reef and steer'. Net braiding was the women's province.

Within spitting distance, on Dock Street was the Fleetwood Navigation School, the brick mission to Deep Sea Fishermen and across at Wyre Dock,

Wyre Dock in 1904: the days when timber and ice came in from Norway.

Net-braiding at Boris Works, once a very necessary industry for Fleetwood girls.

The crew of the dredger Bleasdale, *in the early twentieth century.*

Gourock Rope Works, net braiding premises. Sail makers, ships chandlers and Newton's boat builders with boats in the making on their flagged forecourt.

Prominent were trawler owners' offices, their names a grand roll-call; Marrs, Hewitts, Cevic Steam Trawling Co., Boston Deep Sea Fisheries all overhung with the pungent smell of fish and fish meal. The clatter and clank of dredger *Bleasdale* or perhaps a returning trawler's whistle sounding the haunting 'cock–a–doodle-doo' note would smite the salty air. It was a busy, bustling, emotional, exciting scene. How icy cold the wind on the docks! I once recorded a Fish Auction at 6 a.m. in an October of long ago. I felt like a fish out of water, paralysed with the bleak chillness and mesmerised by the incomprehensible arithmetic of the fish merchants and auctioneers.

In order to bring things up to date it was now my turn to tell Jack of businesses that had risen during his absence.

The leader is without doubt Fisherman's Friend who make the popular lozenges famous all over the world for their extra strong flavour. The company,

The new Lofthouse factory on the industrial estate at Fleetwood occupies 200,000sq. ft of space.

Extra strong lozenges galore!

The Cevic Steam Trawling Company once featured among a grand roll-call of trawler owners. Fisherman's Friend appropriately adopted Cevic FD 241, seen here in Albert Street, with the Pharos lighthouse looming behind.

Fisherman's Friend vintage van off to Norway. The world of Fisherman's Friend embraces Central and South America, North America, South-East Asia, Africa, the Middle East and Australasia.

Lofthouse of Fleetwood, exports to seventy-five countries and has won the Queen's Award for Industry in 1983, 1989 and 1993. Sales teams travel across Europe, Scandinavia and Japan in the eye-catching van. Their new factory on the industrial estate occupies 200,000sq.ft.

One of Fleetwood's oldest trawlers, the *Cevic* FD 7 still appears as trademark on the packaging of Fisherman's Friend lozenges. Built in Aberdeen in 1908 this

Once Lancashire's best-kept secret, James Lofthouse's original formulation of liquorice, capsicum and menthol proved to be a winner. Manufactured in and despatched from Fleetwood, multilingual packaging and the constant visual image make Fisherman's Friend now instantly recognisable worldwide.

Eros against an autumn sky.

Doreen, Duncan and
Tony Lofthouse with
the Lord Lieutenant on
a visit.

The Fisherman's
Friend 'Chattanooga
Choo-Choo' chugs
along Blackpool
Promenade.

Fleetwood at Christmas time. The clock in Fisherman's Walk is in memory of Doreen Lofthouse's mother.

trawler was owned by the Cevic Steam Fishing Co. Ltd and sold in 1953. It is an amazing success story.

Mrs Doreen Lofthouse's love of Fleetwood has led to her generous refurbishment of the Promenade and the purchase of the statue of Eros, a striking figure on its high plinth, welcoming visitors to a marina at Freeport and a lovely, maritime town of unusual interest. Mrs Lofthouse has been made a Freeman of Fleetwood.

Among the many new businesses that flourish are the Buckingham Window Co. established in 1987, the Albert Wilde Pharmacy, James Jackson's Central Garage Ltd, Freebird, John Jenkinson and Builders' Supplies.

It is hoped that the new millennium's gift of years will bring continued good fortune to a town that truly deserves it. Maybe a different type of fortune but one as rich and varied as that which Jack remembered.

Also by Catherine Rothwell

My Lancashire Childhood

Poulton, Thornton & Bispham in Old Photographs

The Lancashire Coast in Old Photographs

Around Clitheroe in Old Photographs

Liverpool in Old Photographs

Fleetwood in Old Photographs

Along the River Kent

SUTTON PUBLISHING

www.suttonpublishing.co.uk